LEAD LIKE
REAGAN

Senator Mike Morrell.

Thank you for your
Service!

LEAD LIKE REAGAN

Strategies to Motivate, Communicate, and Inspire

DAN QUIGGLE

This book is dedicated to my wife, Luanne, who makes life fun and exciting. You are smart and beautiful and an incredible wife and mother. You make all of us better because of your true love for life. You are the most supportive wife a man could ever dream of having and have always been that way. I have enjoyed life's journey because you have made it purposeful and gratifying. Luanne, I love you and appreciate all you do for me and our family. Because of you we have three incredible children, Justin, Corinne, and Eric. Wow. Life is good.

Justin—You are such an incredible son and a true leader in our family. You have not only been a great role model for your brother and sister but also for others. I admire the way you treat people and strive to be your best and I am so proud of all the ways you impact others positively. You will undoubtedly change the world for the better because you have a smart mind, a great sense of humor, a deep compassion for others, and a great love for this country.

Corinne—You are extremely smart and unbelievably athletic, and I am blessed to have you as my daughter. I have marveled at your commitment to your studies as well as the sport you love, volleyball. You are a sweet and loyal sister to your brothers and a good role model to all young women striving to mix academics and athletics. I encourage you to follow your dreams and hope you always know I am so proud to be your dad.

Eric—You have been given a wonderful brother and sister to emulate, yet I enjoy watching you forge your own path. You have been showered with love your entire life and in turn are sharing your loving spirit and good heart with others. Your passion for life is contagious and energizes me. Continue to dream and work hard. The sky is the limit for you!

I've been blessed by a loving and supportive family. I'm humbled and grateful.

CONTENTS

PREFACE

On January 18, 1993, Ronald Reagan's former Vice President and sitting President George H. W. Bush awarded him the Presidential Medal of Freedom, the highest honor that the United States can bestow, which recognizes individuals who have made "an especially meritorious contribution to the security or national interests of the United States, world peace, cultural, or other significant public or private endeavors." I was fortunate to be able to help on that day and was thrilled to have the chance to congratulate Ronald Reagan on that well deserved honor.

Source: The Office of Ronald Reagan photograph by Peggy Grande, Courtesy of the Ronald Reagan Library.

President Ronald Reagan's world-changing power as a leader came not from flexing his political muscle but from an authentic consistency of both thought and action that personified humility, loyalty, and respect. Is this a surprising recipe for greatness? Those around Ronald Reagan felt appreciated by him and connected to him, so they sincerely reciprocated—not only with their loyalty, but with their best work and greatest effort.

This book uses Ronald Reagan, my former boss and lifelong role model, as its primary leadership example. By looking back in history we can see timeless principles in action, which provide a framework for future success and excellence in business and personal life. President Reagan often used stories to make a point or relate to his audience. This book incorporates his stories and speeches, as well as many taken from a wide representation of business leaders and CEOs, and from my own personal experiences. Stories have the power to impact and are used to exemplify what I learned and witnessed.

Imagine how fortunate I was to see at a young age what real leadership looks like. And it wasn't just from the president. It was from the entire team that surrounded him. I am extremely careful to never overstate my position in the office. I was still in college as all of this was occurring, which makes it even more incredible that the opportunity even happened. There I was on February 6, 1989—the president's birthday and my first full day in his office. I was in the conference room with a small group of people singing "Happy Birthday" to Ronald Reagan.

That marked the beginning of a surreal, incredible experience that changed the way I viewed leadership and confirmed all the good things I had thought about the president. Politics aside, Ronald Reagan is remembered as one of the most instinctive, intuitive, emotionally intelligent leaders in recent history. He lived a life of impact—not only on the world stage, but also by investing personally in individuals all around him. As a result, he forever changed my life, and the lives of countless others, for the better.

By looking at Ronald Reagan's leadership style and that of other successful leaders, as well as incorporating my own personal experiences, patterns emerge that make it easy to create a profile of specific traits and leadership maxims that you can implement immediately and that will guide you toward greater personal growth and professional success.

Loyalty and teamwork can accomplish absolutely extraordinary things. Ronald Reagan believed in building people up, not tearing them down. As a result of this dynamic synergy during the 1980s, individuals were inspired and energized, patriotism domestically was renewed, nations were freed, and the world was forever changed.

Whether leading a nonprofit organization, small business, Fortune 500 company, or a family, it's easy to assume that as leaders we should already have all the answers. In reality, our ability to learn, apply, and adapt is what differentiates mediocre leaders from exceptional ones. Exceptional leaders realize that there is always more to learn. The learning process never ends. Learning distinguishes between those who merely do a job and those who pursue excellence, raising up great leaders all around them in the process.

Framing your mind-set for maximizing leadership opportunities yields exponential dividends. Investing in your leadership is an investment in success. It is possible to study examples of effectiveness and learn how to become a great leader, even if it doesn't come naturally to you. You can learn how to motivate and inspire others, set realistic but ambitious goals, and learn to manage and lead your way to greater effectiveness, impact, and success.

There is no question that leaders will always eventually face challenging times. However, when the times get tough, rather than sticking to their vision—their offense—many leaders play it safe, forgoing risk and moving themselves and their businesses into a posture of defense, despite the fact that opportunities still may continue to exist. True leaders will seize and maximize opportunities while others sit on their hands as opportunities pass them by.

According to a study done by The Center for Creative Leadership, 75 percent of careers are derailed or fall short of their full potential due to lack of emotional competencies, not the lack of educational or professional abilities. This void of true, visionary, and authentic leadership has stifled personal success and crippled organizational growth. The inability of some leaders to adapt to change or elicit trust and loyalty from those around them has rendered them ineffective in challenging times.

When I address groups of top CEOs, they agree when I say we hire people for technical ability and fire people for social inability. This is precisely why this book was written. Rather than focusing on the technical necessities for business and personal success, this book illustrates the essential internal and interpersonal qualities that make the difference between simply creating a product and making an impact, between providing a service and providing an exceptional customer experience, between just living life and leaving a lasting legacy.

By applying Ronald Reagan's proven, effective principles and following the examples of successful leaders, you, too, can positively affect performance, as well as the interpersonal environment and overall culture within your sphere of influence. Whether building on what you have already established or confidently starting anew, all is completely possible.

In my own businesses over the past 20 years the same philosophies that President Reagan embraced have inspired me to try to lead like him—to create a vision, assemble a team, communicate a message, lead by example, take action, handle crisis, and ultimately leave the world a better place—all because of Ronald Reagan and his impact on my life.

My hope is that you will be encouraged to honestly evaluate these areas of your life as well, to improve upon your leadership, too—and in reading this book, you'll be inspired to pursue leadership excellence toward your own goals of personal fulfillment and professional success. You, too, can learn to *Lead Like Reagan*. The journey to greater impact begins here.

1 Creating the Vision

Setting Expansive Goals

Our country is a special place, because we Americans have always been sustained, through good times and bad, by a noble vision— a vision not only of what the world around us is today but what we as a free people can make it be tomorrow.

—Ronald Reagan[*]

1

[*]*Source:* Address before a joint session of the Congress on the State of the Union, January 25, 1983.

When Ronald Reagan was sworn in as president of the United States in January 1981, there was widespread malaise domestically. The nation suffered from high inflation, scarce jobs, and low morale. Yet Ronald Reagan immediately took office and began to talk about a new dawn, morning in America, better days ahead, and the proverbial shining city on a hill.

In reality, the country was no different on Ronald Reagan's inauguration day than it had been the day prior. Yet President Reagan proposed a new, ambitious vision, and so America's perception of its own future was entirely, and immediately, different. The images of reclaimed greatness he envisioned for the country made others believe that restoration was possible, not only for the future, but that change was already taking place. America wanted desperately to believe in itself again and in the promise of its future. Through words initially, then subsequently backed up by policy and action, Ronald Reagan made that vision for America a reality.

He was a man of vision and knew how to articulate that vision in compelling, inspiring ways. Ronald Reagan, known as the "Great Communicator," was once quoted as saying, "Most often it's not how handsomely or eloquently you say something, but the fact that your words mean something." He knew that selecting the right words was important, but backing up words with actions was essential. He was successful because he created a vision, articulated the role everyone would play in it, and showed how they would benefit from being part of it.

When the nation faced challenges, Ronald Reagan always refocused on the bigger picture and kept working toward the overall goals and vision. His themes and messages were consistent and clear. Rather than trying to tackle a dozen problems, he focused primarily on two: revitalizing the economy and bringing an end to Communism. He tied those themes into everything he did and everything he talked about, and he kept America focused on those goals, articulating how they fit into his overall vision. As he did, he reminded us of the greatness of which we were all a part, and subsequently, he moved our nation and our world forward, both economically and through the expansion of freedom, realizing both primary goals he had envisioned.

Ronald Reagan motivated the American people to embrace and support his vision for America by inspiring them to share in his desire for renewed pride, patriotism, and prosperity. He connected each one of us to something bigger than ourselves and cultivated a drive and desire to sacrifice as needed and serve and support whenever asked. That created devotion, loyalty, and commitment to an inspired, shared vision.

Ronald Reagan's life and legacy personified vision, both in individual relationships and on the national and world stage. Clarity, consistency, and a contagious optimism filled his words and were validated and reinforced by his actions, both on and off camera.

Painting the Target

The American dream lives—not only in the hearts and minds of our own countrymen but in the hearts and minds of millions of the world's people in both free and oppressed societies who look to us for leadership. As long as that dream lives, as long as we continue to defend it, America has a future, and all mankind has reason to hope.

—Ronald Reagan[*]

I had the privilege and opportunity of a lifetime to work for one of the greatest leaders of our era: Ronald Reagan. Not only was it a personal honor, but it built a foundation for the rest of my life, which gave me a vision of what real leadership looks like—what it should look like and how it is lived out in both large and small ways.

Even when I was a young person, my life was affected deeply by the expansive and inspiring vision of Ronald Reagan. While I was growing up, my parents watched the evening news every night as well as shows that regularly discussed the important issues facing America. I remember being fascinated by the debates and arguments of two unique political viewpoints.

The more I listened, the more I began to analyze not only the message itself but the messengers as well. Some messengers were able to articulate what they believed more succinctly than others. Some were skilled orators, and others would lose arguments I thought they could easily have won. Then in 1980, listening to these differing messages, I was introduced to a man who was running for president of the United States. He looked professional. He looked presidential. He talked to me—not above me or below me—but directly to me, and I hung on his every word.

---

[*]*Source:* Remarks at the Annual Washington Conference of the American Legion, February 22, 1983.

His genuine love for God and country was evident. To me, a new hero was born, a lifelong, substantive hero who represented hope and embodied all that is good about America and the future. The sports stars and superheroes of my childhood were being replaced by a political icon and new personal hero: Ronald Reagan.

I was intrigued by Ronald Reagan and felt invited, included, and needed—as if I were a critical part of his vision for restoring America's greatness. Ronald Reagan's vision was not one just for his benefit; it was for America and the American people—all Americans, even me!

He demonstrated that real visionary leadership is inclusive, not exclusive. Visionary leaders look to build coalitions and connectivity, not isolate themselves from others. Even though at this point in my life I had not yet met Ronald Reagan, I already felt connected to him and to the vision he was articulating. I wanted to be part of it. I believed in it and was willing to become an active participant in promoting the ideas and solutions for America that he was proposing.

I have also had the opportunity to learn from some of the top business leaders in the country, and they have shown me firsthand how effective leaders with vision, those who honestly desire to lead a cohesive, enthusiastic team, can be. Although there are a select few who may achieve success through a condescending leadership style in a punitive culture of fear and directives, the most revered and beloved leaders are usually remembered not only for what they accomplished but also for who they were and how they made those around them feel.

Fortunately, for those of us in the business arena, success in creating an inspiring, compelling vision and a positive corporate culture for a company is not necessarily tied to the product or limited by the actual job itself. Employees of Zappos.com, Chick-fil-A, and In-N-Out Burger can't wait to get to work thanks to the positive corporate culture that exists in those companies. Yet the work itself is fulfilling online orders, making chicken sandwiches, and flipping burgers—jobs we wouldn't typically associate with great personal satisfaction. The employees' enthusiasm is the result of a great, compelling vision and inspiring leadership at the corporate level. People want to be part of something bigger than themselves—and these companies, and countless others, have captured that desire and fueled their success upon it.

Although the application and implementation will be different for each and every company, the goal is the same: To paint a target of success for your company, and even your family, and set your sights on that goal without distraction or diversion.

One good allegory about painting a target for your vision is the story of a world-class Olympic archer. He had multiple Olympic and World Championships and was almost without competition or equal. Like any great champion, he desperately wanted to be challenged, needed to be challenged, and yet rarely was.

One day driving through the countryside, he comes over a hill and sees a barn littered with hundreds of arrows dead set in the center of hundreds of targets. Instead of feeling threatened, he is thrilled and thinks to himself, "Have I finally met someone who can teach me something and provide me with a real challenge?"

He pulls the car off the road and up the driveway to the farmhouse. He knocks on the door, and the farmer answers. He asks, "Is this your barn?"

"Yes it is," the farmer replies.

"Do you shoot?" asks the archer.

"Yes I do. It's a passion of mine," the farmer replies.

"Then I must have the opportunity to shoot with you," the archer enthusiastically responds.

The farmer says, "I would love it—I never get any visitors out here."

They go out to the barn and set up their equipment nearby. The farmer goes first: He pulls back his bow, fires randomly at the barn, then goes and grabs a can of red paint and starts painting a target perfectly around the arrow right where it haphazardly landed!

The true archer watches, deflated in disbelief, knowing that real accomplishment in archery comes only from painting a challenging target first and then carefully taking aim to test your skill. This may be just a story, but unfortunately, many people are just like that farmer and will look at where they started, compare it to where they wound up, and then proclaim that the latter is precisely where they intended to go.

Honestly ask yourself, "Am I randomly shooting with my family? With my personal life? With my professional life? With my business and with other pursuits? Or am I truly painting a target first?"

Without first articulating a clear and inspiring vision, the work becomes just a tedious set of tasks. As a leader, within your company, or within your family, you have to have a reason to get out of bed in the morning and go to the office or go about your day—and so do those around you. Without a clear vision, what are others around you thinking about? For example, on a typical day in a typical workplace, let's say it's 9:30 AM and, likely, people are already thinking about lunch. After lunch, they are thinking about 5:00, and after work, they are thinking about how quickly Friday can come. With clear and motivating vision, those around you are much more likely to stay on task, be committed to results, and pour in their best effort and personal creativity as well—all day and all week long. Someone has to paint the vision first; without it you may survive, but you will never really thrive.

So since we know that people are naturally distracted, here is your opportunity to lead. What is your five-day plan, five-month plan, five-year plan? As a leader, you need to paint the target for which everyone aims and shoots—both individually and collectively as a team.

With my first company, Red, White & Blue Vending, we started with just two machines and quickly built it into a company valued in the millions. We went through 5 five-year plans in five years! It wasn't that we weren't setting ambitious enough goals; it was a result of the unexpected synergy that occurred by having a motivated, dedicated group of employees. Those employees created exponentially more together than they ever could have individually. What a wonderful surprise to experience the power of vision and teamwork, which I had witnessed firsthand from President Reagan and his outstanding staff, and apply it with success in my very first solo business venture!

As a direct result of hard work and commitment to the vision, the team not only achieved each goal, but surpassed them—time and time again! And we were selling candy bars, chips, and sodas. Yet we were all on the same track, moving forward in the same direction. And as a result, we were able to accomplish great things together, regardless of the product line or industry.

When we hit each milestone, gifts were given, parties were thrown, and those who had been instrumental in the achievement of those goals were recognized and rewarded. And at that very celebration, a new vision and new plan were outlined and each person's unique and valuable role in it was defined. Their reward was named, and they were clearly and immediately shown how the vision was both beneficial for them personally and attainable as a team.

This was no different from what Ronald Reagan did time and time again with the American people, which is why I have spent my entire adult life trying to emulate him—to create a compelling vision for myself and those around me, just as Ronald Reagan did for himself, for the American people and the entire world.

Vision in Action

At the root of everything that we're trying to accomplish is the belief that America has a mission. We are a nation of freedom, living under God, believing all citizens must have the opportunity to grow, create wealth, and build a better life for those who follow. If we live up to those moral values, we can keep the American dream alive for our children and our grandchildren, and America will remain mankind's best hope.

—Ronald Reagan[*]

So what is *your* vision? Whether you are leading your family or leading a company or organization, you are being watched.

---

[*] *Source:* Remarks at a White House ceremony celebrating Hispanic Heritage Week, September 15, 1982.

Others want to know what your vision for the future is—because it affects them. If you asked those who you are closest to you what your vision is, would they be able to articulate it? Those around you are listening for the way in which you articulate vision, analyzing whether they think you can fulfill it, and deciding what role they could or should play in it. They are gauging your level of passion or enthusiasm, and based on that, they will determine the level of energy or effort they want to exert in helping fulfill it.

If your leadership history is full of successes, others will be more eager and willing to follow with enthusiasm. Your family, your coworkers, or anyone you lead will rarely be more enthusiastic or more committed to your vision than you are. So create an ambitious and expansive vision, and be ready to promote and advance your ideas with sustained energy, passion, and excitement.

If you are known for having lots of great ideas but not much follow-through, it will be much more challenging to motivate and inspire those around you—but not impossible. It may take a series of small successes to create trust and prove you are capable of maintaining a positive track record. Others will notice your effort, see your consistent achievement, and eventually want to be part of it. It will be contagious if it is sincere—and if the plan of implementation is thorough enough and motivating enough.

Without vision, you drift at the mercies of a constantly changing environment, pursuing day-to-day business with nothing more than a repeated series of activities. Your work becomes like walking on a treadmill, which requires a great expenditure of energy, yet results in absolutely no actual forward progress.

Your vision is what, where, and how you see yourself, your team, or your company in the near, middle, and distant future. It has purpose and structure—a plan and a timeline. It is the main force of motivation. It is what you focus on and rely on when times get tough.

A leader with vision sees the present realistically, as it is, while mapping out a stronger and better future. When written down, communicated constantly and consistently, and shared passionately, a vision unifies a group of people and drives them collectively and effectively toward a common goal. When building a vision, anything is possible—so build it big! Start by identifying your current *what, where,* and *how.* You cannot draw a map to your future without a clear definition of where you are. Next, you need to identify exactly what you want to achieve. The clearer the concept you have, the stronger your vision. Give priority to goals that have true substantial meaning and purpose, or your vision will not survive the first series of obstacles.

Once you know what you want to accomplish, you need to focus your vision by writing out specific incremental steps to take that eventually will culminate in the fulfillment of the overall vision. For each goal, identify the who, how, and when of its completion. Vague goals will never be realized. If the vision is important enough to you, you will find a way. If it is not important enough, you will find excuses. Vision is key, but without a plan for implementation, it will forever remain unattainable.

Next, you need to be able to quantify or measure your vision so that you will know when it has been achieved. Milestones let you measure your progress along the way, and they let you know when to celebrate and reward those who have made realization of the vision possible. It is vital to constantly set new goals to strive for, but it also is essential to celebrate achievement and accomplishment whenever appropriate along the way. People want to feel valued and appreciated—and this is your chance to recognize them accordingly.

Visualize the target for which you are aiming. Everything you do and every action you take should hone your skills, perfect your aim, and get you closer to hitting your target, ultimately turning your vision into reality.

Of course, the future is not one fixed point, and many constantly changing factors and variables can help—or hinder—attainment of your goals. Even in the most carefully constructed plans, there are no absolutes or guarantees. Flexibility and adaptability—essentially the ability to grow and change, even sometimes uncomfortably so—must be woven into the fabric of your personal life and into your company or organization. Where there is no room for change, there will be no room for growth. Do not let a changing landscape discourage you or become an excuse for mediocrity or laziness. Failing to plan is, in essence, a plan to fail.

If our goal is to *Lead Like Reagan*, we must create a compelling vision as he did, setting goals and timelines for action and accomplishment that are ambitious, yet attainable.

★ ★ ★

Creating the Vision

Do you see how the power of one man's vision had the capacity to change an entire country—and then the world? President

Reagan's visionary leadership and optimism for the future not only gave Americans confidence in his capacity to bring about positive change but, of equal or perhaps even greater importance, he inspired Americans to believe in themselves and to dare to dream—and dream boldly—once again. Ronald Reagan led with expansive vision and an optimistic view of the future, a great model for us to follow. He proved that with visionary leadership, anything is possible.

I challenge you to create your vision, take action to fulfill it, enlist support, and take aim, confidently knowing where the target is and having a plan, the skills, and the team to reach it.

Although everyone's exact vision is uniquely different, the power to turn vision into reality is exactly the same.

2 Assembling the Team

Inspiring Loyalty and Commitment

America is no stronger than its people—and that means you and me. Well, I believe in you, and I believe that if we work together, then one day we will say, "We fought the good fight. We finished the race. We kept the faith." And to our children and our children's children we can say, "We did all that could be done in the brief time that was given us here on earth."

—Ronald Reagan[*]

[*]*Source:* Remarks at the Annual Members Banquet of the National Rifle Association in Phoenix, Arizona, May 6, 1983.

R onald Reagan believed that you are only as good as the people with whom you surround yourself. He worked to find the best and brightest people for each area of his administration to create a brain trust around him that would contribute to his ability to make informed, intelligent decisions. He wasn't afraid that he might be outshined, but rather he knew that the key to his effectiveness and success would be having top leaders in their respective fields join him and support him in his vision for America. Rather than being intimidated by those with expertise and experience, he was motivated by it, inspired by them, and thrived on their energy and wisdom.

When Ronald Reagan was elected president of the United States in 1980, rather than limiting himself to people who were already in Washington, D.C., or even automatically rewarding those who had served on his campaign staff or transition team, he committed himself to expanding the reach of his recruitment for his initial cabinet and White House senior staff. He looked for experts across the nation within their various fields. He appealed to their patriotism and persuaded them to give back to their country by sharing their time, their talents, and their expertise with the Reagan administration and work in the White House for a few years, being part of reviving America.

President Reagan did this with great success and was able to bring to Washington, people with unique skills and experiences upon which he would rely heavily and from which he would draw extensively during the challenging years ahead.

By fully engaging and empowering an exceptional team of widely qualified, deeply committed experts, President Reagan ambitiously sought to return America to economic prosperity and pursue the end of oppressive regimes worldwide. He was able to do so with great success thanks to his ability to assemble a team that would be loyal to him and committed to his vision for a revitalized America and a freer world, while bringing their unique and vast experiences to the table.

In a move that surprised many, President-elect Reagan even reached out to James Baker, who had managed the presidential campaigns of both Gerald Ford in 1976 and George H. W. Bush in 1980, both of which had been in opposition to Ronald Reagan's candidacy. Ronald Reagan, though, was able to look beyond any personal aspects of this decision and look to the expertise and effectiveness that James Baker embodied. This proved to be a wise decision, as James Baker is credited with having significant positive influence over the first term of the Reagan presidency, particularly domestically.

Ronald Reagan, using his self-deprecating humor, would be the first one to admit he wasn't always an expert on everything. Yet he would surround himself with expertise, creating a powerful brain trust around him, allowing him to ultimately make informed, excellent decisions.

Through principled leadership and a strong sense of self, Ronald Reagan chose professional value over personal emotion and the country—and the world—benefitted greatly. True leaders are not threatened by having smart people around them; they are empowered by it.

The Value of a Kitchen Cabinet

There is no limit to what a man can do or where he can go if he doesn't mind who gets the credit.

—Ronald Reagan[*]

While he was governor of California, as well as during his time as president in Washington, D.C., Ronald Reagan relied on what he fondly referred to as his Kitchen Cabinet. It was a group of friends and accomplished individuals who were eager to apply their skills, energy, and experiences to advance the goals of Ronald Reagan and his presidency.

This group of 10 to 12 businessmen was composed of strong advocates for the free market system and firm believers in core conservative principles. They provided unofficial advice and personal support to Ronald Reagan from the perspective of business owners, taxpayers, informed citizens, and active participants in the political process.

The people who comprised his Kitchen Cabinet were accomplished, successful individuals in their own right, not nodding, sycophantic yes-men. They were trusted advisors he knew would be tough with him when needed, yet always supportive, even when they disagreed. They shared his vision and were committed to seeing it realized, no matter the personal effort or sacrifice it required.

The difference between mediocre leadership and exceptional leadership often is defined by your ability to cultivate and engage your own Kitchen Cabinet. A true

---

[*]*Source:* Remarks at a meeting of the White House conference for a Drug-Free America, February 29, 1988.

leader recognizes the need to be surrounded with excellence and is wise enough to create an environment where other voices are heard and where advice can be freely given and graciously received.

One example of an environment where this Kitchen Cabinet philosophy thrives is Vistage International. Vistage is a peer-to-peer membership organization for CEOs, business owners, and executives. It helps leaders grow their businesses by aiding in making important decisions and providing a trusted sounding board. Whether you rely on Vistage, a group of friends, colleagues, or coworkers, or an informal group of advisors you have assembled, it is important to realize the value of being a life-long learner, always looking to grow and improve as a leader and learn something new from others.

So who is in your Kitchen Cabinet? Do you even have one? Who should you include? I would look for two to five people you trust and admire and who add value to your life. These people should be willing to be brutally honest with you, share your vision, and be success-oriented. They don't have to be close friends, and maybe they shouldn't be. They may be business associates, mentors, or acquaintances whom you admire. No formal invitation to "Join My Kitchen Cabinet" is required. Just ask them if from time to time they would be willing to let you seek their advice or be willing to share some professional insight and wisdom with you. Discuss big decisions with them. Honestly talk about successes and failures, hopes and fears.

So following in Ronald Reagan's footsteps, I have my own Kitchen Cabinet, which is composed of about half a dozen handpicked individuals whom I trust implicitly for advice and counsel. When I need to make a crucial business decision, I talk to my Kitchen Cabinet. If a majority of them tell me not to do something, I probably won't do it. But if a majority tell me do it, I may take a calculated risk and try to make it happen. I trust and value their various backgrounds, experiences, and expertise to steer me appropriately.

My Kitchen Cabinet is an unlikely collection of individuals and mentors who have been brought into my life in various ways. If they all say *no,* I really listen. As my father used to say, they usually give me "just enough rope to hang myself" if I choose to, but I trust their judgment and their investment in my life and my business enough to tell me the truth, even when I do not really want to hear it or may disagree.

One of my key Kitchen Cabinet members is Ron Bailey. Meeting Mr. Bailey was life changing. His profound influence on my life and in my business is beyond measure. I will forever be indebted to him for believing in me, inspiring me, challenging me, motivating me, and being a consistent example of excellence and wisdom.

In my first business, Red, White & Blue Vending, one of my first large accounts was Strayer University. The office manager at one of the Strayer campuses had gone to a rival Southern California university, the University of Southern California (USC). Having a cross-town rival University of California Los Angeles (UCLA) graduate asking him for business brought him great pleasure.

Nonetheless, he gave me a chance to provide vending services at Strayer's Alexandria, Virginia, campus, which immediately became one of my biggest accounts. I would travel with my route drivers to Strayer and work with them to fill the machines to ensure appropriate product placement and excellent customer service.

While there, I started talking with a man I assumed to be a professor. He would ask me about my business, and I, in turn, would offer him free snacks out of appreciation for his interest and kindness. This went on for months until one day he left the vending area and my USC friend came in and asked me, "What did Mr. Bailey want?"

"Mr. Bailey?" I said. "What does he do here?"

"He owns Strayer!"

The words were barely out of his mouth before I was running down the hallway to catch Mr. Bailey and said, "Mr. Bailey, you own Strayer?" He turned to me, and his response would become symbolic of his humble, genuinely authentic leadership.

"Does it matter?" he replied.

"Yes, it does," I said, "because I want to provide the vending on every one of your campuses."

Again, his response was so symbolic and meaningful. "Then earn it."

"Okay, now you have challenged me," I said.

Within a year I had contracts for all 10 of his campuses and would go on to work with his development team to put Red, White & Blue Vending machines on all subsequent Strayer campuses.

In the years to come, Ron Bailey would become both a trusted mentor and a true friend. He took the time and interest to look over the profit and loss and balance sheets of my company every year. In fact, he really taught me how to read them.

To this day I am grateful for the advice Mr. Bailey gives me and appreciate his serving as chairman of the board for my current business, America's Choice Title Company. We have started other businesses together as well. My life is better in every way for having met him and I am blessed to have him as a Kitchen Cabinet member and a friend.

Finding and Feeding Motivation

I know our people will not fail America. They never have. Our task is to be sure our leaders do not fail the American people.

—Ronald Reagan[*]

For you, as a leader, great effectiveness can come from investing in the personal development of others and finding ways to increase their professional commitment and maximize their tangible contributions. If you can discover what is at the heart of the motivation of others, that is where you will find the secret to unleashing their full potential and engaging their best effort.

Often, motivations may be quite different than what you might assume. I have found in my conversations with CEOs that many of them, and justifiably so, believe the primary reason their employees come to work is for money. Interestingly enough, when I talk to employees within those same companies, the answers from employees vary greatly, but the primary reason they state is appreciation.

---

[*]*Source:* Radio address to the Nation on the Congressional Agenda and the Economy, November 6, 1982.

People are motivated by many different things—maybe they crave appreciation and respect but don't get it at home. Perhaps they are a single parent who is in need of health insurance and that is their primary motivation. It may be their desire for camaraderie or positive interactions with like-minded individuals. Motivations can be as varied and unique as each person.

Learning to identify those motivations in others—and to engage and encourage them uniquely based on their individual motivation—will lead to increased engagement, productivity, and enthusiasm for your overall vision.

By asking questions and really listening to the responses, key motivations can be fairly easily identified. These motivations in and of themselves should not necessarily be seen as right or wrong; rather, it is the process by which you identify and maximize the interest and motivation of others that will ultimately inspire participation and engage productive action.

When I ran my very first business, Red, White & Blue Vending, I was extremely fortunate to have Kirk Murray as my operations manager. He was a hard worker, as loyal as could be, did everything that was expected of him, showed up every day, and was a genuine asset to my organization. I discovered early on that Kirk always gave his best effort, and was motivated by the financial reward which resulted. As a business owner, I needed to find a way to feed that motivation and maximize his commitment while rewarding him in a way that recognized him properly— through his paycheck.

After much consideration and number crunching, I came up with a way to motivate Kirk and sought him out strategically the day before a four-day weekend to discuss it with him.

I said, "Kirk, I need to pay you more money." This statement was predictably met with an ear-to-ear grin.

He responded, "I appreciate your recognizing that. I am working very hard for you. I will do anything you need me to do. So, exactly what kind of money are you talking about?" I could have written a script based on his response because I understood Kirk and the fact that he would appreciate this. He was enthusiastic: "What exactly does this mean? What do you want me to do?" he asked.

"For me to justify this, I need you to be me," I replied. "I need you to care like I do, think like I do, sell like I do, handle problems like I do, and essentially be me when I'm not here. And the reward for that will be that for every day that I do not work in the next year, I will pay you a daily bonus, paid every two weeks in your regular paycheck. If I do not work the entire next year, you will get a 50 percent salary increase. If I work half the days in the upcoming year, you will still get a 25 percent increase."

Kirk was already calculating the numbers in his head—and he loved those numbers. I continued, "You do all the scheduling, ordering, and inventory reports and handle all the problems. However, if there is a problem, you have to tell me. Even if I decide to deal with that particular problem, I will still pay you for that day." I knew it was imperative for him to come to me and be transparent as issues arose and not be incentivized to hide problems from me. I also knew he would think about my offer, and the financial possibilities of it, all weekend long.

When Kirk came into the office on Tuesday morning he set a stack of papers on my desk and said, "You don't have to work for the next three months. Here is the inventory, the orders, the scheduling, and everything else that needs to be done."

I had successfully identified his motivation and found a way to feed it and maximize it. Kirk benefitted, Red, White & Blue Vending benefitted, and I benefitted by freeing up my time to be out selling more and pursuing other personal and professional opportunities. It was a win-win all around.

Another example of finding and fueling motivation involves Christine Micieli, who runs one of my businesses. I am fortunate that she is just as loyal and hardworking as Kirk; however, her primary motivation is not specifically financial reward, it's increased responsibility. Christine is the best of the best. Her knowledge of the industry, her work ethic, and her loyalty are unparalleled.

When the real estate market began its downward slide in 2006, Christine was the first one in my office expressing her concern. She recognized that the market was bottoming out—and quickly. She knew that we needed to start cutting back on expenses—and staffing—immediately.

I sat down with her and said, "You are smart enough to know that times are challenging right now and are going to be so for a while moving forward. As a result, I am going to need you to do something for me. . . . I need you to take on more responsibility. Would you be willing to do that? I would really appreciate it." A small accepting smile was given in response. To my surprise she said, "Cut my salary, do whatever it takes to make sure that we as a company survive. I love this company."

Christine loves the work and the responsibility and authority that come with it. I properly identified her motivation and adequately fed it. Now, of course, I also was fair to her monetarily for assuming additional responsibility and an increased workload. But because that was not primary to her, I did not lead my conversation with her by trying to use that as a primary motivator.

Christine helped navigate through some challenging years in a down market, and her expertise and perseverance allowed us to not only stay in business but continue to grow and expand.

I also remember well a story my father told me about motivation and how he learned the power and importance of it early in his own life. My dad grew up in North Dakota with eight brothers and sisters, all of whom left school around the eighth grade to work for the family's moving business. He never got paid a wage, and even when my father ultimately left home, he was asked to leave his clothes behind for his younger brothers. He worked all that time and didn't even get to keep his own clothes.

With no money, no high school education, and certainly no college education, he joined the United States Air Force. After finishing his commitment, he went to work for Santa Fe Railroad. Eventually he worked his way up to a management position, where one day he had an encounter with an employee who had recently seemed to turn on him and had begun treating him differently—and was becoming very mean and bitter toward him.

My father called this employee into his office and asked him what was going on. The employee said, "Do I have permission to speak candidly to you?" My dad replied that he would expect nothing less, so the man continued. "You give me all the crap jobs. There are a bunch of guys out there, but you give me all of the worst jobs, and I am sick of it. I am fed up with it. I do not deserve it. I work hard for you."

My father started laughing. As you can imagine, this response was not well received, so the employee demanded to know what was so funny. My dad said, "Do you know why I give you those crap jobs? I am so sorry. It is my fault for not telling you sooner, but look at that group of guys out there—not one of them is half as good as you are. I know that if I give you even the most difficult job, that you will get it done. I don't even have to think about it. It will be done thoroughly, on time, and completed in a profes- sional manner. But do you deserve that? No way. So I apol- ogize. I will not let that happen again. Thank you for what you have done so far. I do not know what I would do with- out you."

Silence.

After several moments, the employee smiled and said to my father, "I want you to keep giving me all those crap jobs." He wanted to be the go-to guy for everything. It meant the world to him to have the trust and confidence of his boss, and he was will- ing to work hard to earn it and retain it.

Imagine if you could do this throughout your company, organization, or family: identify and encourage the unique motivations behind everyone's efforts. What kind of family or organization would that create? How efficient and effective could it be if those around you were fully engaged and eager to do their best and were rewarded accordingly?

Where you come from shapes who you are. Everyone is different, and you have a better chance of successfully leading if you can identify motivations and then match them with rewards in that specific direction as much as possible.

By identifying the motivation and maximizing it, the contributions will be greater and the personal investment will be greater as well. It benefits everyone when people grow, expand their own leadership capacity, and succeed personally and professionally. An inspirational leader invests in the betterment of others, uniquely and specifically, helping each one to excel and achieve.

As a leader, if you can find and feed the individual motivations of others, they will work harder, be more loyal, take more initiative, and be more committed to the overall vision.

Just as Ronald Reagan inspired the motivations of ordinary Americans to pursue their own unique vision for their future and contribute to his expansive view for our nation, we can inspire and motivate those around us to pursue personal excellence that will also foster positive motivation and encouragement in others.

Expand Leadership

Surround yourself with the best people you can find, delegate authority, and don't interfere.

—Ronald Reagan[*]

I have hired hundreds of people over the years, which has given me ample opportunity to make some terrific hiring

---

[*]*Source:* Interview with *Fortune* magazine describing his management style, September 15, 1986.

decisions, as well as some that I have later regretted or had to retract. As a result, I have developed in my head a list of the specific traits I look for and value in a potential employee— what I like to call the GOLD Standard.

When evaluating and interviewing potential employees, my goal is to seek individuals who demonstrate four simple traits. My dream employee is known by the acronym GOLD and is characterized by the following attributes:

Gratitude (G) is important for many reasons—people should not just be thankful for the opportunities that life presents, but also grateful for the people around them. They should consistently seek out ways to demonstrate their thankfulness in both word and action. Their life should be characterized by an "Attitude of Gratitude"—a constant awareness of others and appreciation for the ways in which others invest in and contribute to their life.

Optimism (O) is contagious! Ronald Reagan always figuratively viewed "the glass not just as half full, but as overflowing with opportunity." True, authentic optimism permeates everything around it. Like yeast in dough which causes it to rise, a little bit of optimism goes a long way and allows everything around it to rise—creating an environment where anything seems to be— and is—possible.

Loyalty (L) matters. When CEOs talk to me about their employees, one of the recurring themes they are concerned about is loyalty. They want to surround themselves with people who believe in them, who believe in their product, and in the mission or goals of the organization. A loyal employee will work hard to do their best, exhibiting loyalty and enthusiastic support.

Determination (D) is essential. Obstacles are sure to come, but those who are determined to achieve their desired results will find opportunity, not look for excuses to fall back on. I want to surround myself with people who find additional incentives and see the possibilities that exist in the midst of each challenge. Many people assume a victim mentality once they face hardship. I prefer to look within myself to find additional strength and determination when challenges come—and they certainly will. I want those around me to approach life with skill, passion and determination, always expecting the best outcome.

That is it. My dream employee. Why are those simple traits a winning combination? As a leader, you want others around you who are Grateful, Optimistic, Loyal, and Determined. Think of all that could be accomplished if you are surrounded by people who embody the GOLD Standard of excellence in these ways!

Another of my true mentors in addition to President Reagan is the founder of the Leadership Institute, Morton Blackwell. I believe as he does that there are two things to look for in the people who surround you: sustained enthusiasm and the ability to get along with others. Everything else can be trained, learned, taught, or practiced.

People have to want to work through challenges and problems that will surely arise. If they don't have sustained enthusiasm for the task at hand and are not fully committed to the long-term goals and vision, they will not be an asset. They also have to be able to get along with others. It is difficult for adults who haven't learned how to play nicely by now to start learning; you don't want them on your team. If one of these values is missing, that person will be like a malignancy that has the potential to destroy everything and everyone around them.

As an example, one woman in my office would bring in balloons and a present for others on their birthdays—unless she didn't like you. In that case, on your birthday, you got nothing.

People would joke, "I guess I'm on her bad list. Today's my birthday but no balloons or gifts." Yet behind the joking there was an underlying sense of rejection and embarrassment. It became a negative focus within my office, and I ultimately had to fire her because of this, as well as several other reasons. In addition to her unfairness to other employees, she had become toxic to our working environment.

Within 48 hours of that employee's termination, nearly everyone who had worked with her came by my office and thanked me for taking action. Had I allowed her to stay, knowing of her negative effect on others, I would have eventually started losing good employees who did not want to work with her or unwittingly fostered an underground office-wide rumbling of discontent that would undermine our work as a team. Nobody likes to fire people, including me. I once told my business mentor, Ron Bailey, how much I hate firing people. He said, "Good. That tells me you have a soul. But you need to realize that the fault lies with you—not them. Either you (a) did not hire correctly in the beginning, or (b) you did not have enough business in the right area to keep that person in that position." So true, but often hard to hear. Making that decision and ultimately cutting out the toxicity relieves pressure on you as a leader and often improves the energy and morale of your entire team.

In order to avoid hiring the wrong people, we need to learn how to hire the right people, those with sustained enthusiasm and an ability to get along with others and also need to accept the fact that change in the workplace is not always bad. Sometimes you can replace one negative presence with a positive one, and it changes everything else for the better.

The lesson here, though, is fire when you have to, but work hard to hire wisely and surround yourself with the right people in the first place.

I always admired President Reagan's ability to seek out the best, but also his willingness to make the tough and very public decision to fire someone. He desired excellence always and knew that in order to achieve it, everyone needed to be on board and headed in the same direction.

Invest in Excellence

There are no such things as limits to growth, because there are no limits on the human capacity for intelligence, imagination, and wonder.

—Ronald Reagan[*]

Once you have hired well, you need to invest time and energy into those around you in order to add value to their lives, both personally and professionally. From a business perspective, this could mean rewarding long-term employees with additional training. For example, I encourage and support my employees to take the title exam or become notaries. Once I was asked by one of my employees why I was pushing so

---

[*]*Source:* Remarks at Convocation Ceremonies at the University of South Carolina in Columbia, September 20, 1983.

hard for her to become a licensed title agent. I explained that if she ever worked elsewhere, it would be a skill that would add value to her livelihood. She asked, "are you trying to get rid of me?" I responded, "No, I'm trying to help you." She said, "I thought so, but it just feels strange." How sad that she would think it was unusual for someone to sincerely want to help her and provide her with the opportunity to gain a personal and portable skill. And at the same time, she increased her value as part of my team. A true win-win.

Leaders should always look to invest in their organization by investing in the individuals who comprise it. Look for ways to creatively and tangibly build up those around you by investing in the excellence of others.

You can even do things that make others feel special or add tangible value to their personal lives. In my business I have brought in a financial specialist to confidentially help people one-on-one to prepare a balanced portfolio or plan for their retirement. I have also hired a massage therapist for anyone on staff who chose to have a half-hour massage therapy session. One 65-year-old employee approached me privately and told me it was the first massage she ever had. "It was incredible. I loved it—and for the record, you can do that again anytime you want!"

Another time, my daughter and her friend came home after getting a manicure and pedicure, I thought of all of the hard-working people in my office who would probably enjoy the same pampering. The next day, I asked the person in my office who heads up what I call my thank-you department to make appointments for anyone in the office for manicures and pedicures—and as a bonus—my staff was allowed to go during the workday to enjoy this special perk. It was wonderful to be able to reward their dedication with something they truly enjoyed and appreciated.

Your goal should be to build up others around you, making them feel needed, valued, and appreciated. When you creatively and thoughtfully invest time and effort, especially with industry-specific training, you also add value to your leadership portfolio, which adds expertise to your team and overall value to your company. Surrounding yourself with excellence is imperative to success and needs to be cultivated and maintained with great intention.

By always seeking the absolute best individuals to surround yourself with, you increase your effectiveness and your potential for success, growth, and excellence. By celebrating and taking pride in the success of those around you and looking for ways to build them up, you are opening up limitless possibilities for them personally, and for your team collectively. Weak leaders are threatened by smart, savvy people, whereas real leaders thrive on surrounding themselves with excellence, being personally challenged to always improve, and ultimately wanting the best for themselves and for the team.

★ ★ ★

Assembling the Team

Once the vision has been created, the right team needs to be assembled. It is an essential component of bringing personal and professional goals and dreams to fruition.

Those around you need to know they are an integral part of your team, because they are. If they were not essential, then you wouldn't and shouldn't surround yourself with them. The measure of your own success is, after all, ultimately based on their success. So choose wisely, identify primary motivations and feed them, encourage professional development, support personal growth, and celebrate all that can be accomplished by a motivated, fully engaged team.

Put the right people in the right positions, not based on years of association or friendship, but based on your assessment of how they truly add value to you and to the overall vision, uniquely strengthening and enhancing the team. By identifying strengths (using GOLD, for example), assembling the right team, growing professionally, and adhering to your core principles, your overall success and ability to motivate others dramatically increases.

Do you have a Kitchen Cabinet? Have you started thinking about those who can be part of one? If not, identify and engage one of your own. By learning from Ronald Reagan and his example of how to assemble the best team, you can inspire loyalty and earn and keep greater commitment from those around you, culminating in increased personal and professional success.

3 Communicating a Message

Connecting Others to Your Vision

I won a nickname, The Great Communicator. But I never thought it was my style or the words I used that made a difference: It was the content. I wasn't a great communicator, but I communicated great things, and they didn't spring full-bloom from my brow—they came from the heart of a great nation—from our experience, our wisdom, and our belief in the principles that have guided us for two centuries.

—Ronald Reagan[*]

---

[*]*Source:* Farewell Address to the Nation, January 11, 1989.

With predictable humility, Ronald Reagan talked about his nickname the Great Communicator—and attributed greatness to the American people, not to himself. Ronald Reagan truly never saw himself as better or as more important than anyone else, and regularly gave credit to others. He understood the importance of effective communication and consistently and masterfully displayed what it looks like at its very best.

A clear and expansive vision was the essential foundation for all that was accomplished during the Reagan presidency and is the fundamental component to all achievement and accomplishment. Yet without a way to communicate and articulate your vision, it will never be built upon or develop into a reality. It requires the support, the enthusiasm, and the efforts of those who are affected by its direction and will be affected by the fulfillment of it. Articulating and communicating vision in inspiring ways can make the difference between overall success and utter failure.

Ronald Reagan had an intuitive way of connecting with people—which is the essence of all communication. The words he used were vital, yet their ability to accurately connect with the intended recipient was imperative. He knew that without a personal, emotional connection to what was being said, the message could not make an impact or bring about change.

Ronald Reagan was successfully able to connect with individuals of every age, race, demographic—and even political party. Regardless of your politics, you could not have disliked Ronald Reagan after meeting him. Every person who crossed his path felt noticed by him, appreciated by him, and valued by him. He exuded warmth, graciousness, and a casual familiarity, while still maintaining the dignity of the presidency and the power of the office. Even his public communication captured an essence of personal connection that led to his overall effectiveness.

Many years before I personally met Ronald Reagan, his impact on my life was already great. When he spoke, I felt, even as a young boy, that he was talking directly to me. Somehow he was able to connect with me in meaningful and powerful ways. From the first moment I heard him speak, I knew that I wanted to learn to communicate like Ronald Reagan.

In the 1980s, I was a stereotypical high school athlete and gave little thought to being able to captivate an audience like Ronald Reagan could. Yet life sometimes takes interesting, unexpected twists, and just before my junior year, a new debate coach came to San Gorgonio High School in San Bernardino, California.

The debate coach's attempts to recruit me for the debate team could only be described as extremely persuasive—or perhaps coercive. He had heard of my high esteem for Ronald Reagan and would ask me about it repeatedly. Although I appreciated his interest, I certainly could not see myself as being part of the debate team at my high school. After several brief hallway encounters, he cornered me and said, "Dan, if you ever want to be like Ronald Reagan, if you ever want to speak like Ronald Reagan, if you want to be able to fight for and articulate the principles that Ronald Reagan represents, you must join the debate team."

I had no choice but to eventually say, "Yes!" That was the overwhelming power of his persuasive communication. It turned out to be the right decision—one that affected not only my remaining two years of high school, but one that set me on a path toward my future in ways I never could have anticipated. As a result of my success on the high school debate team, I was subsequently offered a scholarship to debate in college as well. I declared my major as political science and continued to build on the foundations of debate established in high school and was blessed to learn under the first-rate tutelage of Dr. Bob Rivera when I went to college.

The technical training in the mechanics of speaking, debating, message creation, timing, and delivery were vital to learn. I will forever be grateful to Dr. Rivera for giving me the tools I would need later in life to articulate a vision and connect others to it.

Vision is the foundation, and communication is the vehicle by which your vision starts to take shape and come to life. Passion for your goals and commitment to the end result are the fuel that drives you forward, even when the road is challenging. Although your particular vision, communication style, and passion will be unique, there are common traits and themes that are evident in examples of successful, memorable, and effective communication in action.

Ronald Reagan never used any sort of system or program to articulate his vision. He spoke plainly and genuinely to the American people—from his heart and with genuine sincerity about what he believed was best for America and for the world. He appeared to be a naturally gifted communicator, and in his adult life, he certainly could be considered as such. Yet in his youth, Ronald Reagan was shy and introverted. His foray into the spotlight first began in church, where he participated in community readings with his mother, and of course later, as an actor in Hollywood, where his communication was developed, refined, and embraced as a natural part of his persona.

Although many are blessed with this gift, I believe that effective communication can be learned by everyone and traits of meaningful, memorable communication can be mastered and applied by anyone who is willing to devote themselves to practice and growth. Ronald Reagan is certainly an excellent example of such diligence and ultimate success.

Memorable Messaging

> *General Secretary Gorbachev, if you seek peace, if you seek prosperity for the Soviet Union and Eastern Europe, if you seek liberalization, come here to this gate! Mr. Gorbachev, open this gate! Mr. Gorbachev, tear down this wall!*
>
> —Ronald Reagan[*]

While examining effective communication, I wanted to highlight and acknowledge one of Ronald Reagan's greatest speeches—and perhaps one of the most unforgettable speeches of all time—the speech he delivered at the Brandenburg Gate in Berlin on June 12, 1987, and show how he masterfully wove elements of meaning and memorability seamlessly together.

Not only were his remarks that day eloquent and powerful, but Ronald Reagan's speech, which boldly challenged General Secretary Gorbachev to "Tear down this wall," was a great

---

[*] *Source:* Remarks on East-West Relations at the Brandenburg Gate in West Berlin, June 12, 1987.

example of brilliantly communicated and visionary, principled leadership. In part, this speech inspired and unleashed a series of events that ultimately changed the world for the better in tangible and lasting ways.

This speech demonstrates the potential power, dynamic results, and lasting impact of words–not only for those who heard the speech that day, but for all who have heard it since. I believe that his example can be emulated by anyone who desires to communicate with lasting results and is committed to success.

During that now-famous speech, Ronald Reagan certainly recognized the significance of his message, the location of its delivery, and the implications it could have on the lives of millions of people, specifically across Eastern Europe. The significance was enhanced by the substance, which was intended to challenge and confront the Soviet Union and empower and inspire those affected by Soviet influenced oppression.

Ronald Reagan's passion for bringing about the end of Communism was well known and began back during his years as president of the Screen Actors Guild, where he was influential in leading and navigating others through the Red Scare in Hollywood. For decades he had been boldly speaking out against Communism, so there was no doubt that his remarks in Berlin that day were full of sincerity and passion. His convictions and emotions were on full display as he carefully and purposefully articulated with firmness and certainty his desire to expand freedom's light. He fervently believed in what he was saying and in what he wanted to accomplish.

His vision and call to action was defined by four short words: "Tear down this wall!" Succinct, memorable, relatable. It was easy to understand what action he was demanding from General

Secretary Gorbachev. The call to action was loud and clear with no ambiguity.

Although not specifically used in the Brandenburg Gate speech, Ronald Reagan often used stories to illustrate his vision, communicate his main message, or provide examples of success or inspiration. Personal stories from his own life, or stories shared with him by others were often the core of his remarks, interwoven with facts, historical significance, and themes of patriotism. Likewise, on this particular day in Berlin when the stakes were high and the message was intense, he did not have his memorable big smile, which he typically wore.

Although advised against saying those now-famous words, "Tear down this wall," Ronald Reagan knew, based on his personal understanding of General Secretary Gorbachev, that it was the right approach and that being "politically correct" would not have been as effective or memorable. Sometimes against advice, a leader needs to "get mad on purpose" and express emotions in appropriate ways that will stir others to action and response. This is exactly what he did that day in Berlin—and did so with lasting, memorable impact.

Ronald Reagan led with a vision he was convinced was right, even against opposition. Although it was considered risky by some to confront Gorbachev and the Soviet Union so overtly, in his heart he knew it was the right thing to do, regardless of how it was perceived. He felt that the possible consequences of this verbal challenge were far less grave than the consequences of not articulating the challenge—and he was right. With those four words, the challenge was laid and the rest became history. What would have happened if Ronald Reagan had stayed silent and played it safe? Thankfully for Eastern Europe and for freedom-seekers worldwide, we will never have to know.

Communicating with Impact

> *They called it the* Reagan Revolution. *Well, I'll accept that, but for me it always seemed more like the great rediscovery, a rediscovery of our values and our common sense.*
>
> —Ronald Reagan[*]

In studying the highest levels of leadership, impact, and influence, several common aspects of effective communication become clear. Ronald Reagan masterfully demonstrated their application in his speech at the Brandenburg Gate, and you can apply these same key components as you plan and create your own messaging. Powerful communication skills are critical to positively affect the overall direction and impact of your vision and its fulfillment. Here are 15 essential ways you can increase your communication success:

1. *Significance.* Realize the significance, the power, and the importance of clear, concise communication and the effect it can have on others and on the fulfillment—or the failure—of your vision.

2. *Substance.* Have substance—something meaningful and important to say. There are many leaders today who talk more and more and yet say less and less. Know what you want to say before you start talking. Plan your communication with great intention.

---

[*] *Source:* Farewell Address to the Nation, January 11, 1989.

3. *Sincerity.* Communicate with honesty and authenticity— with sincerity. The more sincere your message is, the more impact it will have on others. You need to choose your vision carefully and make sure it is one that you wholeheartedly embrace and can communicate genuinely.

4. *Sell it.* Believe in your vision and in your message. You need to have more enthusiasm for your vision than you expect others to have. Your passion and energy, or lack thereof, will be evident to your listeners.

5. *Say it.* Tell your listeners what you are going to tell them, then tell it to them, then tell them what you told them. Make sure they leave knowing exactly what you want them to know and remember.

6. *Say it again and again.* Constantly refer to your vision. Have a consistency in your message over time, every time you communicate. Make it clear to others what you stand for, what you believe in, and what your vision is. Repeat it. Retell it. Restate it. Repeat it.

7. *Symbolize it.* Personify your vision, and symbolize it. When you think of Ronald Reagan, you think of freedom. Make sure those around you know exactly what your vision is— and then personify it with consistency.

8. *Stance.* Be aware of your stance: 55 percent of face-to-face communication comes from body language, 38 percent comes from tone of voice, and only 7 percent of communication actually comes from the words used. Your nonverbal cues speak much more loudly than your words, so learn to control and manage your body language and facial expressions, making sure they match your spoken message.

9. *Specialize.* Even though you may be articulating your vision over and over again, it will be more meaningful and memorable if the message is customized for those hearing it— specialize. You should talk to people at their level, not over their heads or beneath them. Talk to them, specifically.

10. *Study.* Be prepared, study, be informed and well read, and have compelling, arguments supporting your vision. You should know more about your subject matter, your industry, your plan, and your vision than anyone else. Research related topics and fields so that you have an expansive base of knowledge. Gather relevant facts and information and develop creative ways to share them.

11. *Style.* There are many effective methods of speaking, so find your unique style. Infuse your personality, your background, and your vocabulary into a personal cadence and rhythm of speaking that uniquely suits you. Practice articulating your vision. Ask for candid feedback and continue to hone your most effective style.

12. *Simplify.* Use small, short words that everyone can understand and remember. A simple message clearly articulated is much more effective than one that seeks to impress others with your knowledge but is not able to transfer any of that knowledge to others.

13. *Solicit.* Invite commitment and support. When you communicate, it should be clear what is being asked. Articulate your vision and outline the role you want others to play in fulfilling it. Do not assume they know what you are asking of them. You have to tell them—and then persuasively invite their support and their best efforts.

14. *Stories.* Combine your content with original stories and personal examples that are meaningful to you and relevant to your vision. Stories can create far greater impact than just a conveyance of facts, ideas, or opinions. Chosen carefully, stories can affect others in powerful ways.

15. *Smile.* Nothing is more effective in engaging others than a genuine smile when appropriate. It brings a transparency to your message and conveys a warmth and kindness that has the potential to disarm even the harshest critic. Open the lines of communication by smiling—it is contagious!

Although there is no magic formula to becoming a Great Communicator, in your own way you can formulate, articulate, and communicate your vision with greater success, effectiveness, and confidence.

★ ★ ★

Communicating a Message

As we see from Ronald Reagan, making memorable remarks is one thing, but those who are able to spur others to action, invite active participation, or cause a positive change in thinking or behavior truly understand the value and importance of communication. Words without action are without impact. Ronald Reagan, time and time again, not only spoke words with resonant meaning and impact but prompted action from the American people and the world.

Ronald Reagan communicated ideas, thoughts, goals, and a vision that others embraced and acted upon—using many of the characteristics of communication excellence listed in this chapter. For you, whether it's a keynote speech or a casual conversation with a family member, the true meaning and value of effective communication can be realized through focusing on the listener and tailoring your message accordingly. If you want to really improve the way you communicate and the impact your messages have on others, look over the previously mentioned characteristics and see how many you currently incorporate. What else should you include? Are you regularly evaluating what you say, how you say it, and how your words are being heard by others? If you truly want to communicate like the Great Communicator, you need to challenge yourself to embrace additional aspects of communication excellence.

Whether you are communicating a vision to your company or speaking to your family, my challenge to you is seek to make an impact, not just make a point. Following the example of Ronald Reagan, choose your words carefully to inspire action and change your world and the world of those around you.

Ronald Reagan showed that once created, a vision communicated with substance, passion, and style can change the world. It has before and can and will again.

4 Leading by Example

Using Emotional Intelligence to Model Excellence

A leader, once convinced a particular course of action is the right one, must have the determination to stick with it and be undaunted when the going gets tough.

—Ronald Reagan[*]

---

[*]*Source:* Address to Cambridge Union Society, December 5, 1990.

P resident Reagan strategically and wisely took great strides to develop personal relationships with other world leaders, which would help manage the complexities of his foreign policy and build a unified front against aggressors. He was a staunch believer in face-to-face diplomacy and believed that alliances could be forged, or differences could be resolved, if two leaders sat down face-to-face and talked to each other.

Despite initial differences and even overt confrontation, Ronald Reagan's eventual personal, warm relationship with the Soviet Union's General Secretary Mikhail Gorbachev was a prime example of what could be accomplished if two people, originally suspicious and skeptical of each other, were willing to talk—in person. Ronald Reagan pushed for this because he honestly believed, and was right to assume, that even among the vast differences that marked them politically and personally, there had to be a few small areas on which agreement could be reached.

Rather than focusing solely on extensive disagreements, Ronald Reagan reached out to Gorbachev with the few elements on which they could agree—that nuclear war was a war in which there could be no winner and the reality that increasing the Soviet military would also dramatically and rapidly increase the demise of the overall Soviet economy. From that meager starting point, much was added, built, and ultimately agreed upon, including the signing of the INF Treaty and the beginning of the end of the Cold War, and ultimately the fall of the entire Soviet Empire.

Another example of seeking support and building alliances for his goals and vision was the great triad of power and influence that Ronald Reagan vigorously cultivated between Prime Minister Margaret Thatcher, Pope John Paul II, and himself. This collaboration was key in putting pressure on the collapse of Communism, beginning primarily in Poland, where Pope John Paul II already had great connectivity, respect, and a loyal following among Polish Catholics. The three leaders could apply greater influence and accomplish greater change together worldwide than they ever could have gained independently or regionally. Working together, they chiseled away at Soviet resolve from their unique positions of influence, and the foundation of Communism was weakened and ultimately could no longer stand. Slowly, steadily, consistently, it was pushed back from a variety of fronts thanks to this united trio.

Even in the 1980s, as debt crises spread across Europe, many of the G7 leaders also looked to the United States, wondering if the newly implemented tax cuts of the early 1980s and Reagan's corresponding deregulation would be effective. Although skeptical at first, and mocking many of these "crazy American ideas," Chancellor Helmut Kohl of West Germany watched with amazement at how quickly the American economy recovered during Ronald Reagan's first term, and he soon implemented many similar policies in his country.

As president, Ronald Reagan was a skillful builder of coalitions. Across political aisles and with unlikely partners, he was able to identify potentially supportive groups and individuals and nurture their support of his goals and vision. Using appropriate and often self-deprecating humor and having a strong sense of self, Ronald Reagan was able to neutralize negative groups. He saw his vision as always being one of addition, not one of subtraction. He wanted others to see the value his goals would bring them and highlight their common interests, not emphasize the differentiating details that perhaps might encourage further divide.

He expansively reached out to groups and individuals with a potential interest in his vision and then determined which ones he could successfully influence to be included among his supporters. He articulated his vision in such a way that they believed that his success would also contribute to their own success. America's victory would be their victory as well. Including others in the creation and fulfillment of his vision was essential in both earning support and prompting action. Seeking to include, not exclude, expanded Reagan's base of backing domestically as well as abroad.

Taking a page from the playbook of Ronald Reagan, we should realize the wisdom of looking for ways to find agreement and build upon that first. Rather than exaggerating and highlighting differences with others, which only defensively drives each to their respective corners and makes compromise nearly impossible, we should seek first to find agreement, collaboration, and win-win solutions that will lead to real results and enhance success.

Earn, Don't Demand Loyalty

*The way I work is to identify the problem, find the right individu-
als to do the job, then let them go to it. I've found this invariably
brings outs out the best in people. They seem to rise to their full
capacity, and in the long run you get more done.*

—Ronald Reagan[*]

Your influence as a leader should not be based on coercion or
blind compliance. The goal is to earn sincere and genuine loyalty
as a leader so that others will be inspired by it, committed to it,
and contribute to it. Loyalty born and built upon respect and
trust will not only be gained and retained but is more likely to be
sincere and passionate.

Your leadership should lend itself toward effectively persuad-
ing others to participate in the completion of tasks, culminating
in the accomplishment of a specific goal. In other words, as a
leader you should be able to motivate and inspire others to do
something, not just inspire them to believe something.

From a sheer organizational standpoint, what are some of the
reasons that would motivate others to participate in your vision
and the work surrounding its implementation? One reason might
be that they perceive you to be in a position to reciprocate the
favor on an equal or greater level. This is, however, less effective
than other methods because it depends on your role or perceived
power within the organization, which can change and therefore
alter or remove your effectiveness to wield this type of influence.

The more effective way to earn support and apply influence
is to appeal to a shared value or concern. If others care about

[*]*Source:* Address to the Nation on Iran, March 4, 1987.

something you are championing or advocating, they will be more likely to be loyal to you and support your efforts. The key is to build allies, starting with those who share your passion or conviction. If they genuinely share your beliefs, they will be a loyal follower of your vision and participate in the process of implementation.

Inspiring others through your leadership is far more effective than leadership by edict.

Dream Sharing

I've always believed that a lot of the trouble in the world would disappear if we were talking to each other instead of about each other.

—Ronald Reagan[*]

Nearly every opportunity I have had in life began with someone else helping me. Some may call it calculated luck, but I call it "dream sharing" and honestly believe that if you tell enough people, share your dream enough times, position yourself appropriately, meet the right people, and do the work necessary to prepare, you can wait for "the luck part" to kick in. Results come from hard work—and a little dream sharing.

Virtually everyone who knows me has heard me dream share. I cannot help people if they do not share their dream with me—if they do not tell me where they want to be—and they cannot help me if I do not share my hopes and dreams with them.

---

[*]*Source:* Remarks at the Ford Claycomo Assembly Plant in Kansas City, Missouri, April 11, 1984.

Dream sharing is not the same as networking. When you network, you look for people who can benefit you or your business. When you dream share, you make an intimate connection with another person with a desire to help them, regardless of whether it can be reciprocated.

Instinct and Emotional Intelligence

There are no constraints on the human mind, no walls around the human spirit, no barriers to our progress except those we ourselves erect.

—Ronald Reagan[*]

The buzz in the corporate world recently has been emotional intelligence. Leading research institutions across the nation continue to present factual, statistical evidence supporting what many of us already know—academic and intellectual knowledge, in and of itself, is not enough to produce a successful leader. Instinct and intuition are required for excellence, not just technical skills and training.

Such studies serve only to underscore the emotional and relational traits that mark the difference between a mediocre leader and an effective leader with lasting impact. Some studies even suggest that up to 75 percent of the competencies that set apart the average leader from the outstanding leader come down to social and emotional intelligence, not academic intelligence. It is the outstanding leader who genuinely inspires others to wholly commit to a unified, collective group

---

[*]*Source:* Address before a Joint Session of the Congress on the State of the Union, February 6, 1985.

goal and inspires the contribution of their complete individual potential at the same time.

Long before there was the term *emotional intelligence,* there was an emotionally intelligent leader named Ronald Reagan. A fortunate few are born with similar emotionally intelligent traits of leadership. For the rest of us, we can be learn, practice, and thoughtfully integrate these traits into daily life, both professionally and personally.

Many companies have discovered the hard way that just because an employee has been successful in sales or another department, it does not automatically make that person a great manager of others. Leadership requires emotional intelligence, interpersonal wisdom, and savvy in navigating the intricacies of relationships within the business environment.

Although there is great variation on the technical research-based characteristics of emotional intelligence, we are going to discuss it here in a general sense, defining it as the ability to read, anticipate, and modify or control the emotional response and actions of yourself and others.

Intuitive Leadership

> *The greatest leader is not necessarily the one who does the greatest things. He is the one that gets the people to do the greatest things.*
> —Ronald Reagan[*]

A person's overall intelligence and level of ability goes far beyond his or her IQ. There is a personal and a social component

---

[*]*Source: 60 Minutes* interview with Mike Wallace, October 18, 1975.

in addition to test scores or academic performance that either contribute to or undermine a person's overall individual success and leadership effectiveness.

Acknowledging and navigating the complex personal challenges of managing your own emotions and actions, along with identifying and understanding the interpersonal intricacies of relationships with others, are key components of your ability to build coalitions, earn loyalty, and make insightful decisions. The initial focus for managing others should be an introspective look at how you are currently managing your own life, your own emotions, and your own actions.

How in tune are you with yourself; how do your staff and others view you? To put it humorously, let me ask you this question: Do you have CEO disease? Regardless of whether you are the president, an executive, a vice president, manager, or team leader, or a parent, after a conversation, do you walk away thinking, "They love me and they think I am hilarious!" All the while, however, the people you just finished talking to are thinking, "I'm sick of hearing about his golf game because I could never play golf with all of the overtime I put in here. I am sick of hearing about his 80-foot yacht because I do not have one—and never will. I am sick of hearing about his kids in private school because I could never afford to send mine to private school on the amount of money I'm paid."

We spend so much time critiquing others throughout the day, but when is the last time we turned the mirror onto ourselves to see how we are perceived by others? Unfortunately, you may not like the initial impression you see in the mirror.

Self-examination and management begins with a willingness to candidly examine how you are perceived by others. Are you recognizing and appropriately responding to the cues that others are giving you? Without taking this to the extreme or becoming oversensitive to every word or look, you need to be aware of your environment and your place and your role in it. Although you cannot and should not constantly bend to the whims and opinions of others, you do need to be aware of what others think about you so that you can manage from an appropriate framework and know where the starting point is for your leadership.

If you question your ability to accurately self-assess, be willing to seek feedback from trusted sources. You can simply say, "I am trying to be the best leader I can be and need help to get there. What should I do more of? Less of? Add?"

Integrating input from others into your life is much like trying on a new coat. It may fit and be exactly what you need. Or it may need some adjustments to be a good fit for you—take it in a little bit, let it out a little bit. You may also "try on" that feedback for a while and decide that it's not quite right for you. You have to be willing to adapt to lead more effectively, but you need to know where your leadership stands in the first place, and that can come from the feedback of others.

I personally do this, even with my family, and it has worked well over the years. Sitting down with my oldest son, I said, "I want to be the best dad I can be. How am I doing? What can I do more of? Less of? Add?" He once answered, "You know that joke you tell about me all the time? Don't do that. It is embarrassing." I replied, "All right. I'm sorry. You won't ever hear me say it again." And he never has.

The same question asked to my youngest son had slightly different results. He said, "You could give me ice cream all the time." This time, however, that request was not granted; being a good, loving, responsible parent would not result in providing ice cream 24/7 to my son, although I did applaud his creative attempt.

When you ask those three questions, and wait patiently for the response, what do you think that does to you and the relationship with that other person? It strengthens it because they feel their input is valued and their relationship is important to you. They are part of your improved leadership and have become a trusted contributor to your growth.

Periodically step back and judge your progress and your performance, and identify your strengths and weaknesses. Pinpoint what is moving you forward and what is holding you back, and celebrate your progress. Take pride and satisfaction in the process, not just in the result. Positively affirm your efforts and your achievement.

There are many diagnostic tools you can use for objective evaluation, but your best feedback will likely come from those around you who are invested in your leadership success and are willing to be brutally honest with you. If allowed to speak candidly without recourse, the people around you can be influential and essential in encouraging you in your personal growth and expanding your leadership effectiveness and excellence.

Strong Sense of Self

We Americans have never been pessimists. We conquer fear with faith, and we overwhelm threats and hardship with courage, work, opportunity, and freedom.

—Ronald Reagan[*]

---

[*]*Source:* Radio Address to the Nation on Economic Recovery and National Defense, December 18, 1982.

Ronald Reagan had a great sense of self and used an appropriate amount of humor, often self-deprecating, to break uncomfortable tension, make a serious point in a memorable way, or defuse a hostile opponent. He would often take an accusation aimed at him and turn it into an acknowledgment of the criticism, while not embracing the ill-will or the substance behind it.

One well-known example took place during the 1984 presidential campaign debate between Ronald Reagan and Walter Mondale. Mondale was trying to imply that Ronald Reagan was too old and tired to be an effective president for another four years, yet Ronald Reagan successfully defused the issue of his age by responding, "I will not make age an issue of this campaign. I am not going to exploit, for political purposes, my opponent's youth and inexperience." Many think that was the moment in which Ronald Reagan's reelection was secured. The audience roared with laughter, and even his opponent was unable to contain his amusement over the president's reply. Ronald Reagan had enough self-awareness and self-confidence to acknowledge those who were skeptical of his advancing age, yet he deflected that concern in a way that was humorous, surprising, and politically disarming.

Morton Blackwell, founder of the Leadership Institute, often says, "Don't make the perfect the enemy of the good." Many of us, especially within leadership roles, make perfectionism the enemy of our own achievement or accomplishment. Although we should continually strive to do our best, and then a little bit more, the all-or-nothing, critical, unrealistic, and defensive tendencies of the perfectionist within often works against us. Do not allow a fear of failure—or falling short of the perfect result you desire—keep you from moving continually and consistently forward toward your goals and vision.

If you believe in yourself, don't take yourself too seriously, allow humor to play a role in your life and don't "make the perfect the enemy of the good," you ultimately can achieve greater leadership success.

Drive toward Success

> *I, too, have been described as an undying optimist, always seeing a glass half full when some see it as half empty. And, yes, it's true— I always see the sunny side of life. And that's not just because I've been blessed by achieving so many of my dreams. My optimism comes not just from my strong faith in God, but from my strong and enduring faith in man.*
>
> —Ronald Reagan[*]

You have just one shot at life—why not make it great! Beyond just meeting your own standards of excellence, there should be a desire to exceed personal goals and tangibly reach and surpass professional goals. Successful and sustainable leadership is ultimately impossible without this progression. Setting impressive, lofty goals is admirable, but without the drive and desire to actually implement, achieve, and surpass those goals, they are just theory, not reality.

While focusing on yourself, you need to see beyond the details of the day-to-day operations and visualize a bigger,

---

[*]*Source:* Ronald Reagan Library opening ceremonies in Simi Valley, California, November 4, 1991.

better future for your business, your team, your family, and yourself, and work tirelessly toward it. Go above and beyond the standard expectations, and focus on the next step once that work is done. Press for ongoing innovation, and be willing to take calculated risks. Do not work for the sake of working; work harder, longer, and smarter toward a specific goal, then reevaluate, refocus, and move continually onward, personally challenging yourself to learn, do, and achieve more.

On your drive toward personal success, don't allow emotions to derail your efforts or undo everything you have worked for. Although emotions have great influence over us and can often override our intellect, work diligently to maintain appropriate control over them and do not allow them to control you.

Sometimes the most effective emotional response may be to show anger or displeasure, but even then you should get mad only on purpose and do so on your terms and with appropriate restraint. You can remain in full control of your emotions, yet use an emotionally charged response to elicit attention, response, and action. It is important to not allow emotions to drive you, but to always drive your emotions toward action and success.

Empathy toward Others

They say the world has become too complex for simple answers. They are wrong. There are no easy answers, but there are simple answers. We must have the courage to do what we know is morally right.

—Ronald Reagan[*]

---

[*] *Source:* "A Time for Choosing" Speech, October 27, 1964.

Regardless of how self-aware or introspective you are and how much you invest in your own personal development and growth, ultimately your leadership capacity will be determined by your ability to engage, motivate, and inspire others.

An example of the importance of this occurred recently when Christine, the vice president of one of my companies, asked to see me, and I was shocked at how upset she was. I had never seen her this way. She said, "There is a closing that was going to happen this morning, but the man I am supposed to be closing with cursed at me for an hour on the phone last night. He said things that no person should ever say to another human being. I do not have to put up with that. There is no way that I'm going to do this closing. Period."

I replied, "Christine, we are in a tough market. You need to go close that deal. Be professional and close it," and I walked out to attend an off-site meeting.

I left the building, got in my car, and had driven about 200 feet down the road before I pulled over. Christine had been unfailingly loyal to me since day one. She had never refused any task set before her. I had been so focused on the closing and, yes, the money we stood to gain from it, that I had completely disregarded her thoughts and feelings about the hurtful way she had been treated. I immediately felt over-whelmingly sick about it.

I could not dial my cell phone fast enough and called her from my car. "Christine, first of all, please accept my deepest apology. I support you 110 percent. Nobody is going to treat you that way. I will call the guy right now to let him know why we are not going to be closing this deal today—and why we will refuse to do business with him anymore."

There was silence. Christine then said, "I'll close the deal."

I said, "I don't think you understand, you don't have to close the deal."

She responded, "I perfectly understand. I will be professional and make it happen."

I offered to turn the car around, cancel my meeting, and stand outside the conference room door. I told Christine, "If he even looks at you wrong, if he makes your blood pressure rise, stand up, leave the closing, and I will physically escort him from the office."

Her response was, "Okay, thank you."

So I immediately turned my car around and went back to the office.

What did Christine really want? She wanted support, she wanted empathy.

And your ability to be aware not only of what others are doing and saying, but what they are feeling, is crucial to your success.

As leaders, we deal with people, not robots, so we need to include emotional awareness in our management of others if we want to connect more effectively with those around us.

Situational Awareness

Now, what should happen when you make a mistake is this: You take your knocks, you learn your lessons, and then you move on. That's the healthiest way to deal with a problem.

—Ronald Reagan[*]

---

[*]*Source:* Address to the Nation on Iran, March 4, 1987.

Responding appropriately in every situation requires an ability to assess and gauge all the underlying dynamics, backgrounds, and even the unique cultures that are different in every environment.

I was talking about this at a conference, and when I got to this point, one of the participants took issue. He said, "Dan, we live in this politically correct world where you cannot freely say anything. I am fed up with it. I am just going to be who I want to be."

I said, "Okay. Fair enough."

Interestingly, his daughter was a participant in the meeting as well and was about to be married. I walked over to her and said, "I hear you are getting married next month. Congratulations. You must be very excited." Then I asked, "Would you be candid with me for a moment? Are you at all concerned about what your father might possibly say over the four-day period surrounding your wedding that may embarrass you or your friends?" The dead silence that followed got her father's attention.

"Are you worried I will embarrass you?" her dad asked.

"Well, Dad, you do tell some off-color jokes sometimes when it is not appropriate."

Her father was stunned. Moments ago he wanted the freedom to say whatever he wanted to, but he didn't realize that sometimes what he said was embarrassing or hurtful to those he loved—primarily his daughter. Sometimes being who you want to be and saying what you want to say may not come across how you intend and may be perceived in a way that alienates and isolates others.

Awareness of the unique environmental dynamics will help you determine when it is appropriate to say or do something—

and who it is appropriate to do so in front of. This is not just for the benefit of others; it is essential for your growth as an effective, respected leader.

Ronald Reagan intuitively had an innate ability to appropriately assess the dynamics of a situation, which was exhibited in many ways, even in his sense of humor. He was a great storyteller and always had a joke or a lighthearted story to share with his guests and visitors. Yet even in those situations, there were jokes or stories he would share only in groups of men and those that he knew were appropriate to share in front of women, too. Although none of the stories were in and of themselves inappropriate, he always carefully selected what he would say in mixed company versus what he would tell when he was just "one of the guys." And the impressive part was that even when it was "just the guys," he always remained a true gentleman, appropriate and respectful.

We, too, should be careful to monitor what we say and the words we use, ensuring that our words don't detract from our ability to lead and earn loyalty from others.

Timing and Approach

Things like faith, love of country, courage and dedication—they are all part of the inner strength of America. And sometimes, they do not become self-evident until there is a time of crisis.

—Ronald Reagan[*]

Within any group there is power that lies outside of the official head of the organization. Learning to identify and tap into

---

[*]*Source:* "A Time for Choosing" Speech, October 27, 1964.

those unofficial power sources shows great intuition and will pay dividends often beyond what can be accomplished through the standard chain of command.

I once met with a philanthropist who had amassed a fortune in excess of $4 billion. The goal for this particular meeting was to secure a half million dollar donation for the nonprofit organization I was representing.

I walked into his 2,000-square-foot personal office, which had three separate rooms and a putting green. There was a giant flat-screen TV behind a massive desk with stock information streaming by. I introduced myself, thanked him for taking the time to see me, and asked how he was.

He responded, "I don't know. Two of my businesses that were doing $500 million last year are doing only $200 million this year. Two more are in bankruptcy, but one is treating me mighty fine, so I guess I'm doing good. How about you?" What an introduction!

A few courtesies were exchanged, and we began discussing the purpose of my visit.

"I know you genuinely believe in the mission of our organization as your support has been unfailing. For that we are grateful. Today, though, I would like you to consider a very generous donation of $1 million to continue to build our programs." Then I stopped talking. At that point, the first one who talks loses, right? He knew that as well, and we both just looked at each other. I was in no hurry. I had all day—and the view of downtown was breathtaking.

Finally, he said, "You did not just ask me for a million dollars! What is my biggest donation so far? $250,000? No. There's no way. I'll give you half a million. Not a penny more."

Doubling his largest donation was extremely generous, and was exactly what I had been asked to secure, but it was still short of my own personal goal of what I thought was possible. I said, "Let me just send you a proposal. All I ask is that you look at it before making a final decision."

"All right. You can send me a proposal, but I make no promises."

I thanked him for his time, and on the way out, who do you suppose I talked to about that proposal? His personal assistant. His gatekeeper. The person sitting right outside his office all day every day. Why did I talk to her about it? Because she is in the closest proximity to him and in a position of extreme influence over his time, schedule, and decision making. I had taken the time to get to know her as well, not just her boss. I had built a rapport with her in the months leading up to the meeting. I recognized and acknowledged the position of power she held. She knew it and appreciated my recognition of her influence.

I said, "No one knows your boss better than you do. If you were sending over a proposal that you wanted to be well received, when would be the best time to send it?"

She said, "Hmm. Interesting question. No one has ever asked me that. I would send it over at 8:45 AM on Thursday morning. He gets a financial report every Thursday morning about 8:00 AM that always puts him in a good mood."

The following Thursday morning I had my e-mail ready and was counting down the minutes until 8:45 AM when I could send it. The organization ultimately secured the $1 million donation because I understood and applied an awareness of the power structure and the importance of timing within that organization.

I understood who made the decisions and who had the most influence and not only recognized those factors at work but maximized them for beneficial good.

I once told this story to a group of CEOs. One of them raised her hand and said, "I just had an ah-ha! moment. I just lost a major deal because I was selling to the owners and they were not the ultimate decision makers—it was the manager who made all the decisions. And I had ignored the manager."

In politics, in business, and in life, it's important to identify the ultimate decision maker because your success often is based upon your ability to do so.

Ronald Reagan didn't always want a diplomatic attaché negotiating on behalf of him and his administration. Whenever possible, he believed in the value and benefit of personally getting in front of the actual decision maker himself to negotiate and directly make his point to those with the power to influence and affect change.

Trust and Teamwork

Peace is not the absence of conflict, but the ability to cope with conflict by peaceful means.

—Ronald Reagan[*]

Teamwork is the unified efforts of a group of people toward the accomplishment of a common goal. Depending on the type

---

[*]*Source:* Remarks at Eureka College Commencement Address, Eureka, IL, May 9, 1982.

of business you are in, teamwork may or may not be essential for base productivity, but sustainable growth cannot ultimately be achieved without employing and mastering it.

As a leader, you must function on two levels of teamwork, unifying your subordinates and gaining their loyalty while working effectively among your peers and other leaders as well.

Facilitation of teamwork is impossible where there is no trust, collectively and individually. Not only must there be account-ability for the team as a whole, but its members must be individ-ually accountable as well. You must cultivate a consistent environment of respect, tolerance, and loyal interdependence throughout your organization in order to foster teamwork and camaraderie.

Although numerous companies and facilities are exclu-sively dedicated to team-building experiences, enhancing the bond between employees does not require elaborate or expensive activities. In my office, we have held our own Office Olympics with events we designed ourselves and paper plate award ceremonies. In less than five minutes on the Internet you can discover hundreds of activities from which to choose, which will enhance your team's engagement with one another and build a stronger, more unified team of employees.

This is not meant to be just playtime and fun and games. It is an investment in the development of trust, mutual respect, and possibly even friendship among your team members, all of which will strengthen their trust in one another, increase their loyalty to your organization, and ultimately solidify their commitment to your leadership and vision.

Beyond the team as a whole, as a leader you need to invest individually in each person who makes up that team. Peggy Noonan was one of President Reagan's most notable speechwriters. It has been widely told that the first speech she ever wrote for him was supposed to be five minutes in length. She has said that she expounded on her given topic for 15 pages, and submitted it for his review. President Reagan crossed out a majority of it, handed it back to her, and said, "I love it. It is a great speech. Thank you."

Discouraged, Peggy turned to one of the veteran speechwriters and said, "He said he loved it, but he axed everything! The majority of it is gone. There is practically nothing left! And this was good work."

"Well," said her colleague, "you have just been 'schooled' by Ronald Reagan."

President Reagan would never beat a person down. He always took what he was given and found the good in it, even if it was only a small percentage. Peggy Noonan was smart to take her "schooling" and examine closely his comments and apply them to future writings. She realized that she learned more by looking at what he had left in her speech than by focusing on all that he had taken out.

Peggy Noonan ultimately accepted—and valued—Ronald Reagan's ongoing praise for her efforts and moved forward successfully to help him craft some of his most memorable remarks.

The Great Communicator brought the best out of a new staffer, inspiring her to become her personal best and one of his most valued assets, while also accomplishing his goals. By extending respect to her first and showing appreciation for her work, President Reagan enabled Peggy Noonan to add further respect, power, authority, and credibility to his presidency by helping him to communicate greatness through his speeches and public statements.

★ ★ ★

Leading by Example

Beyond intellect and the ongoing pursuit of knowledge, true leaders need to expand their intuitive leadership and realize that instinct, insight, and inclusion will also play key roles in their growth and success. My challenge to you is to examine and evaluate your emotional competencies and learn to manage your actions and emotions, having awareness and sensitivity toward others. Dream sharing with others expands opportunities for helping others achieve their goals and dreams, while also potentially inspiring participation in your own personal and professional vision.

Ronald Reagan modeled the synergistic power of creating alliances with others and showed the contagious optimism of successful implementation of policies that work. He demonstrated the importance of maintaining control over his emotions, using them when and how he chose, and he also showed us the greatness that can result when you invest personally in the lives of those around you as an emotionally intelligent leader.

Anyone who works with other people realizes the value of emotional intelligence. Great leadership requires much more than education—it demands emotional and relational traits.

Do you show empathy? Have situational awareness? Strive for inspirational leadership? By elevating your commitment to being the best leader you can be, and seeking ways to improve your emotional intelligence, not just your technical ability, you can expand your capacity to model excellence and inspire excellence in others through leading by example.

5 Taking Action

Turning Ideas into Achievement

Let it never be said of this generation of Americans that we became so obsessed with failure that we refused to take the risks that could further the cause of peace and freedom in the world.

—Ronald Reagan[*]

[*]*Source:* Address before a joint session of the Congress reporting on the State of the Union, January 27, 1987.

President Reagan came to office with a vision of expanding freedom, both domestically and abroad. He wanted to get government off the backs of American businesses and unleash the American entrepreneurial spirit. He also wanted to expand freedom and liberty worldwide. Anything that didn't fit into this simple framework would not be a top priority for him or his administration.

Ronald Reagan's faith and core beliefs were essential to providing him, and the country, with direction and guidance throughout the 1980s. He believed that America was unique in the world and that it was the role of limited government to serve its citizens, not the other way around. To President Reagan this meant helping those who truly needed it and getting government out of the way for the vast majority who just wanted the freedom and liberty to pursue their own unique American dream.

In many ways, the economic challenges of the Reagan presidency had been over a decade in the making. Some blame the policies of Richard Nixon, including wage and price controls. Others trace it back even farther. Either way, by the time President Carter led the country, we had a misery index (inflation plus unemployment) of more than 20 percent. The country was dejected and looked to President Reagan to take quick and decisive action—to help lead the country forward as he had ably led California as its governor for eight years. They wanted a leader who would guide them out of malaise and back into a proud, restored America with a vibrant economy—and they found it in President Reagan.

Immediately, he took action, to face head-on and reverse the previous economic policies that relied on the redistribution of wealth or Keynesian stimulation. Although these policies had temporarily and artificially boosted the economy in the past and in concept had sought to help those in need, they did not succeed in expanding the volume of wealth or providing sustainable progress for those who needed it. In other words, some people were better off, and some people were worse off, but the average number of those who remained impoverished and in need remained unchanged. In addition, the economy was struggling, stagnant, and discouraging to private sector businesses and their potential growth.

Although the concept of supply side economics had been around for a while, the idea of lowering the cost/burdens on the "suppliers" of goods so more could be produced less expensively, had its first large-scale test under President Reagan's leadership. By making it easier for suppliers to produce goods, they hired more people and sold items for less. The entire market grew and benefitted as a result. Although many critics initially mocked the idea, supply side economics, which also became known as Reaganomics, became an unstoppable force for growth and expansion once it was unleashed on the American economy.

This not only accomplished President Reagan's goal of reviving a struggling economy and restoring America's confidence in it, but also fit within his undying belief that less government was preferred and that freedom, when given the chance to flourish, is always best for individuals and society. And he was right—it benefitted our nation economically and collectively.

Setting Priorities

This country was founded and built by people with great dreams and the courage to take great risks.

—Ronald Reagan[*]

President Reagan set an ambitious agenda to accomplish while in office; however, he wisely limited his promises to a few key areas and therefore was able to deliver on the things he promised. Ronald Reagan demonstrated the importance of having an overarching framework of goals and then taking action accordingly.

As a leader, everything you do should fit into the established guidelines of what you believe and the primary leadership goals you want to achieve.

Regardless of your available resources, it is almost certain that you will never be able to accomplish everything you want to as a leader. True leadership requires establishing priorities and focusing limited resources in a few strategically selected directions. Focusing on fewer items makes it more likely that the ones you pursue will actually succeed.

I was fortunate to learn early on from President Reagan the importance of staying focused, taking action, and being decisive based on specific, predetermined priorities. This came into play for me personally when I was exploring the possibility of expanding my company into multiple additional states. While I was in the midst of that consideration, but before I did so, the economy took a sudden and dramatic downturn. This forced me to shift

---

[*]*Source:* Remarks to Massachusetts High Technology Council in Bedford, January 26, 1983.

priorities and become more valuable to a smaller group of customers locally and regionally. In the end, I was far more successful in narrowing my focus to a specific group of customers rather than trying to expand my customer base and risk jeopardizing the high level of customer service I was giving to my existing customer base, especially at a time when the market was so unsteady and volatile.

Take Action as a Team

> *Today we did what we had to do. They counted on America to be passive. They counted wrong.*
>
> —Ronald Reagan[*]

Although President Reagan often had to change his method of implementation, he didn't compromise on his core principles. On top of maintaining momentum toward the overall goals, this practice also allowed the entire team to act consistently and in sync with the key objectives.

An effective leader needs to delegate tasks and relinquish control over much of the implementation and needs to become comfortable with not knowing exactly what is being done by every employee every minute of the day. By clearly and consistently articulating a simple set of guiding principles, you are more likely to get the desired outcomes from the efforts and contributions of others.

Your team will also be more motivated to take action because they will be empowered to act, and they will do so with the

---

[*]*Source:* Address to the Nation on the United States Air Strike against Libya, April 14, 1986.

confidence that their decisions are consistent with your overall vision and goals. Businesses often struggle and many fail, not because they had bad ideas, but because they kept changing direction or were inconsistent in choosing or communicating their core principles.

In large organizations, it often takes years to get a new idea fully implemented. If the leader is reorganizing or changing course constantly, the last idea may not have had time to be fully implemented or reach its full impact before something new is introduced. This tendency for change at too rapid a pace can create fragmentation in your company because some will be working toward your last vision, while others are already moving on to your next. It also can cause a lack of commitment to your ideas because employees will think that it isn't worth their time to invest in this plan because another, different one is just around the corner. However, frequently changing course in the face of changing market conditions is necessary and can be successfully accomplished if you have long-standing ties to strong core principles, such as excellent customer service or cutting-edge innovation.

Even as my company has gone through tremendous adaptation in the size and scope of our products, our clients were confident that our steadfast commitment to exceptional customer service would not change—and it didn't. As competitors allowed their service to suffer, we ensured that we continued to do whatever it took to make—and keep—the customer happy. In some cases, that even meant that we reduced our expected return; however, we still maintained our key principles and our corporate culture, which gave our company stability even as we were forced to make drastic changes in a rapidly evolving business climate.

When the market started to come back, our loyalty to our customers was rewarded as they honored us with more of their business and referred countless other clients to us.

To be successful and accomplish your goals, everyone has to be moving in the same direction. Whether it's your company, your family, or your organization, you need a mission statement and goals, and an ambitious, yet attainable, plan of action to ensure that your goals are realized. A confident, professional, and unified team is unstoppable.

Implement the Plan

> *May each of you have the heart to conceive, the understanding to direct, and the hand to execute works that will leave the world a little better for your having been here.*
>
> —Ronald Reagan[*]

Every aspect of implementation will require a precisely coordinated team effort. There will certainly be elements of implementation that you will have personal responsibility for, such as vision creation and ongoing direction and communication, but the coordinated efforts of a team are essential.

Break tasks up into workable objectives and assign someone to be responsible for each one. Every task needs to be given to someone who will be accountable for its completion. Be specific in your designations. Otherwise, as the adage goes, "if everyone is responsible, nobody is responsible."

_____

[*]*Source:* 1992 Republican National Convention in Houston, Texas, August 17, 1992.

Building the needed infrastructure, assigning appropriate responsibility, and procuring the necessary resources are absolutely required to succeed.

The quickest way to success is by modeling success. Just as those around you will learn by your example, you should also seek out advice and wisdom from those who have already been successful and learn all that you can from their example. Learn from their best experiences, practices, and ideas. This will give your team great confidence that the goal is achievable and that confidence will translate into swift and purposeful action. There is no better motivator toward solving a puzzle than knowing someone else has already solved it, and proving that a solution exists.

By the third year of Ronald Reagan's first term as president, it was clear that it indeed was "Morning in America" again. The turnaround had started as just a U.S. phenomenon, but all over the world and especially in Europe, prime ministers and chancellors were looking for solutions to their economic challenges and began to follow the example of Ronald Reagan. As a result, by emulating America, many of their economies also began to revive and thrive.

Even the Soviet Union took notice and soon realized that its own economy was crumbling and would not be able to compete or keep up with a resurgent United States, militarily or otherwise. Not only was Ronald Reagan's commitment to peace through strength based on bolstering military capabilities, but he knew that economic stability and strength were equally important. By rebuilding both the domestic economy and restoring the U.S. military equipment and forces, additional political pressure was put on the Soviets. The weaknesses of

Communism showed mightily in the contrast to the vibrancy of a proud and renewed United States. The Soviets watched one by one the collapse of politically oppressive regimes world-wide and symbolically were dealt a devastating blow with the fall of the Berlin Wall. Ronald Reagan's prophetic words—that Communism was destined for "the ash heap of history"—were indeed coming true.

In contrast, China noticed these changes as well but chose to continue with its Communist political controls. However, it did eventually begin to slowly pattern its economic growth based on a Western capitalist model to try to keep pace with freer economies worldwide.

Ronald Reagan's actions matched his words, which were all part of his effectiveness in achieving his vision. Likewise, your steps should lead toward active implementation of your plan.

Most plans are made up of countless individuals and carefully coordinated actions. During a project's implementation, your job as a leader is to maintain the proper course, set an appropriate pace, and keep everyone's enthusiasm high. Even a president faces distractions during the day and needs to continually refocus, reguide, and remind those around him or her about the priorities, goals, and big picture—the vision. President Reagan could have lost enthusiasm for his goals of reviving the economy and putting an end to Communism, but instead he continually articulated, communicated, and gave voice to his vision, which not only kept him focused but inspired those around him.

Leaders need to model the appropriate amount of enthusiasm and effort. Rarely will those on your team have more enthusiasm for the project or vision than you do. You need to be the trailblazer, the pacesetter, and the cheerleader all in one for your team. People respond well to a leader who is consistently enthusiastic and invests in the projects at hand. Those around you want to also feel inspired to pursue those goals with confident enthusiasm and active support.

In any plan, mistakes will be made. Although those mistakes will typically be quickly corrected, it is your response to those mistakes as a leader that will endure longer than the error itself. If you support the team, even in times of failure and encourage them to learn from their mistakes, confidence and creative energy will continue to grow. If you lose your temper or blame, punish, and belittle employees publicly for their mistakes, everyone else will be watching as well; the result will be more hesitant decision making in the future and an unwillingness to contribute any innovative ideas or make decisions that might be perceived as risky.

Activating the energy of those around you also releases more of their creativity. Every plan experiences unexpected challenges ranging from internal conflict, external opposition, or a change of circumstances or environment. Sometimes, it is possible to just press on through trying times, but sometimes that is not the right solution. In fact, pressing on, especially in the face of opposition, often creates more resistance. Creative solutions are required and will be provided by those who feel free to submit ideas and participate in problem solving without criticism or dismissal.

And, of course, no plan is fully complete without following up. You must have hard facts to know whether you are making actual progress toward your goal. Most of all, you need to judge when the overall plan, or elements of it, need adjustment.

President Reagan had resources available to help him monitor progress, yet he still needed to be the driving force behind accountability, progress, and direction toward his goals. For urgent crises, the White House's Situation Room has become famous. Secure, top-secret, real-time global information streams come together for a core group of decision makers who take immediate, decisive action. Although the Situation Room often sees conflict that demands swift response, it has also been used to help divert or defuse domestic and international conflict through withholding retaliation. As leaders, it is good to remember that sometimes no response and no action are the better choices.

Although not everyone has their own Situation Room, the concept is the same when applied to business. You will be able to make the best possible decisions when you collect all pertinent information, gather educated, wise supportive voices and take decisive action based on the resources and knowledge you have available to you.

Assess and Adjust

Trust, but verify.

—Ronald Reagan[*]

Turning around the world's largest economy after a decade of malaise was President Reagan's top priority. He met with his team on the economy right away, developing both a short-term plan of action and a long-term vision of fulfillment and imple-mentation. Ronald Reagan knew that a leader should not focus exclusively on either. Long-term achievement rides on a series of

---

[*]*Source:* Interview with Alastair Burnet of the U.K.'s ITN Television, March 10, 1988.

short-term successes. Keeping that in balance means being able to quickly and appropriately respond in real time, while not losing sight of the overall objective. Your job as a leader is to do both, keeping in mind that there is no long term if you don't successfully take care of the short term right now.

For each critical project in your overall plan, make sure you keep a regular pulse on its status. In some cases, this could be daily or weekly. Keep the updates efficient by addressing issues and soliciting input.

When possible, you, as the leader, should keep everything coordinated, but step out of the limelight and allow others to collaborate and work among themselves. Don't become an obstacle to the projects and sabotage their progress or success.

Sometimes assessment will determine that no adjustment is required—sometimes you need to stick to the original plan. As mentioned earlier, President Reagan's famous line, "Tear down this wall!" almost wasn't uttered. He stuck to his original intent and put those words back into the speech countless times after others, including people in the State Department, continuously removed them. He took a risk, made the statement, and prayed for the desired effect. Staying the course meant changing the world.

Pursue Efficiency

If you're afraid of the future, then get out of the way, stand aside. The people of this country are ready to move again.

—Ronald Reagan[*]

---

[*]*Source:* Remarks at a Virginia Republican Party rally in Richmond, Virginia, September 29, 1982.

President Reagan believed that in order to get government out of the way of the American people, he had to improve efficiency in the federal government by reducing or eliminating as much of the bureaucracy, regulations, and paperwork he could. In the 1970s, federal bureaucracy had its hand unnecessarily in a variety of industries. As one example, there was an appointed federal official who not only set airline fares but also decided that peanuts should be served on flights. For those old enough to remember, flying in the 1970s was both expensive and very inconvenient. These federal rules and regulations not only drove up costs for existing airlines but also were a significant barrier to innovation within the industry and discouraged expansion of the industry itself. Airlines trying to get into the aviation business at that time had difficulty doing so, and those already in the business found it challenging to merely survive.

Under President Reagan, the elimination of much of the bureaucracy at the federal level quickly unleashed a wave of innovation across the country, not only for the airlines, but across all industries. Once there were fewer rules to follow and regulations to abide by, businesses could get back to focusing on their customers, on growth, and on innovation. In that way, not only did President Reagan have a huge impact on the federal government, but he also triggered a domino effect of enthusiasm and entrepreneurialism across the entire economy, creating exponential growth nationwide.

In the business world, top influential CEOs were taking similar action in igniting growth and expansion in their companies by stripping away unnecessary layers of oversight and overbearing bureaucracy within their companies.

In any market it is advisable to pursue efficiency—while still maintaining high standards of excellence and doing what is right. By maximizing efficiency, it is possible to create expanded output, gain greater market share, and potentially increase profits, sometimes even with fewer resources. If you carefully consider areas where you can become more efficient and rally others around doing more with less, you'll be surprised how this unleashes a huge amount of productivity when motivation, enthusiasm, and incentive are abundant.

In 2006, the economic downturn necessitated the downsizing of many businesses, including mine. I had to find ways to become more efficient, including reducing the number of offices and the number of employees. Our fast response to the dramatic and threatening changes in the business environment saved the company and retained the jobs of the remaining individuals. The advantage for my company was that once I was forced to streamline my staff, everyone that remained was a top performer. Had we stuck to the vision and goals that were created under different circumstances and not acknowledged the changes we needed to make in response to the evolving business environment, then the company would have been completely lost. Eliminating bureaucracy and overhead expenses and streamlining the efficiency of our operations kept us afloat through difficult times and prepared us to grow again when the economy improved.

Once the real estate market stabilized but before it really started expanding, we were already positioned to grow our business again because we had learned to be more efficient.

Our streamlined operations also allowed us to offer lower prices than our competitors and made us more resilient for the next inevitable downturn. As painful as it can be to live through, this process of pursuing efficiency can potentially make businesses better, stronger, and lowers costs to customers. The process of regularly analyzing your business to look for duplication, waste, or excess is vital to staying competitive and relevant in a constantly changing business environment.

Challenge the Status Quo

> *Heroes may not be braver than anyone else. They're just braver five minutes longer.*
>
> —Ronald Reagan[*]

President Reagan embraced his role as a change agent. That role started with making sure everyone was committed to the magnitude of the challenge ahead. Every one of us has a preexisting idea of what we believe is possible and impossible. There are even things that we know are necessary, but we honestly don't believe they can be changed. The economic catastrophe of the 1970s caused a lot of people, including many government leaders, to give up precisely when the country most needed them to show resolute, visionary leadership.

Those who lead with lasting impact are able to think differently than the rest of the industry and the competition. If you want a different outcome than the status quo, then you need to do things differently, and that means beginning to think differently.

------

[*]*Source:* Remarks at a Virginia Republican Party rally in Richmond, Virginia, September 29, 1982.

In his book *The Science of Success*, American entrepreneur Charles Koch, says that in order to stay competitive, it requires that "a business apply the processes of experimental discovery and creative destruction to its vision, strategy, products, services, and methods. All businesses must constantly innovate."

In essence, the success of Koch Industries is based on the creative destruction of their operations. In other words, they rip it apart and put it back together—all in an effort to ensure that they do not become stagnant, but remain as efficient and successful as possible.

So when, oh when, was the last time you did "creative destruction" on your personal life, your professional life, and your business? Last week? Last month? Or last year? Or maybe you haven't done it in over 20 years? The reason why we do what we do today is usually because we did it yesterday. My challenge to you is to take action by practicing "creative destruction" on a regular basis to stay competitive.

The most obvious business example comes from a company that actually used the slogan "Think Different." As we play our music while texting friends on our smartphones, it's difficult to remember that the company credited with inventing the personal computer almost failed. It had to bring back its founder, Steve Jobs, to resurrect the entire company, restore its vision, develop creative problem solving, and reinspire an expansive and successful future of growth, innovation, and profitability.

As with Ronald Reagan, much has been written about Steve Jobs. He had three secrets to business success: understand customers better than they sometimes understand themselves; stay relentless in your visionary pursuit of efficiency; and, most important, understand that you need the team to think differently, and therefore shed the restrictions of the past and invent your own future.

General Electric championed the slogan "Find a better way, every day." Even if you are confident in the solution you want to implement, you should still constantly challenge the status quo and think differently every day. We all need to immediately do things differently if we want to move forward.

I'm not a physician and I don't possess specific knowledge of medical equipment, but a friend of mine who is a trauma surgeon complained about needing to use several different pieces of equipment in order to perform a few basic tasks. Through brainstorming with him on how to simplify this process, we ended up developing a groundbreaking multiuse product called SmartShears. You can learn more about Medix SmartShears at www.medixmedical.com, but in essence they are an autoclavable, 4-in-1 device that includes trauma shears, a reflex hammer, a ruler, and an angle. Their efficiency saves money, and their accuracy saves lives. This cost-effective tool has streamlined emergency departments and trauma work. Medix SmartShears are a result of challenging the status quo and thinking differently—and the medical community and the patients they serve are benefitting as a result.

The reality is that most ideas fail long before they are imple-mented. Whether it was a bad idea to begin with, there were insufficient resources, the plan for implementation was flawed, or the timing was unfortunate, some ideas are bound to die along the way—and that's okay. Failure clears the way for the best ideas, to survive and receive sufficient resources and successfully be implemented. In fact, as a leader, one of your most critical jobs often isn't deciding what should be done but rather sometimes deciding what should not be done.

President Reagan faced great adversity and challenges both at home and abroad during his presidency. Although he stayed true to his principles, one of the things that made him a great president was that he constantly adjusted his implementation. He challenged his team to always look for new, innovative alternatives to business as usual.

A great example of his ability to think differently was seen in his approach to fighting the Cold War with the Soviet Union. Ronald Reagan believed that we should defeat them from a position of strength. Declaring the Soviet Union an evil empire, he initiated an arms race that could not be won by the economically challenged Soviets. In the personal meetings between President Reagan and General Secretary Gorbachev, it became clear to Gorbachev that this was a war that should not be fought, because it could not be won. Due in large part to President Reagan's efforts, the Cold War eventually came to a peaceful end. Prime Minister Margaret Thatcher, of the United Kingdom, said of Ronald Reagan, "He won the Cold War for liberty and did so without a single shot being fired." This was the "Think Different" slogan personified. Ronald Reagan was able to win a war without ever having to actually engage in combat.

★ ★ ★

Taking Action

Ronald Reagan created a vision, assembled his team, communicated the message, and led by example, but ultimately to be successful in tangible ways, he had to be willing to take action, make a decision, show backbone, and stand strong for the things in which he believed passionately in bold and ambitious ways.

Real leaders practice "creative destruction" regularly, ripping the status quo apart, and putting it back together in ways that are more efficient and, ultimately, more successful.

Ron Bailey, my Kitchen Cabinet member, says, "as a leader you need to ultimately make a decision—and in order to be successful you need to be right most of the time." Whenever he says that, I laugh and think, "No pressure . . ." but if we know that is the truth, then to be successful in taking action we must set our priorities and make sure we are focusing our efforts in the right direction. We must take action as a leader, but appropriately engage those around us and inspire them to action as well.

You need to pursue efficiency, making sure that you are not adding an unnecessary layer of bureaucracy that will limit the forward movement of your plan. To actually implement a plan, you need to outline and articulate the necessary steps to make it successful, pressing forward through any obstacles, distractions, or frustrations that arise. Ultimately, you must be willing to challenge the status quo and do things differently.

We know from playing and watching sports that a coordinated team can accomplish far more than even the most talented individual can accomplish alone. Your business and your family work the same way and you, as the "head coach," need to assemble the right team, prepare, and be ready to take action and implement a winning game plan.

6 Handling Crisis

Finding Opportunity in Challenges

No crisis is beyond the capacity of our people to solve; no challenge too great.

—Ronald Reagan [*]

[*]*Source:* Remarks at the first Conservative Political Action Conference (CPAC) in Washington, D.C., January 5, 1974.

"It CAN Be Done"

Ronald Reagan kept a sign on his desk with four simple words, "It CAN Be Done," that were symbolic of his belief that in America anything was possible and that we were limited only by our own dreams. Ronald Reagan's personal contentment, humility, and undying confidence in the goodness and spirit of the American people helped the nation believe in itself again, motivated its spirit, and restored patriotism and incentive toward growth, innovation, and entrepreneurship.

"It CAN Be Done" inspired him and others to persevere, regardless of how daunting the task, ambitious the vision, or challenging the implementation. As president, Ronald Reagan knew that many decisions would be tough and often agonizing. Implementing those decisions would be equally as difficult, but "It CAN Be Done" inspired him to press on with hopeful resolve.

As president, Ronald Reagan delivered countless famous speeches and created numerous memorable moments. So why are many of the events we remember and point to as defining moments of his presidency born of sadness, tragedy, or disaster? We recall the *Challenger* disaster, the bombing of the Marine barracks in Beirut, and his emotional speech given to the Boys of Pointe du Hoc in Normandy, France. We remember not only his words but also the emotions within us that his words evoked.

He demonstrated true leadership, even in the midst of tough, disappointing times in our nation's history. Each time, his remarks to the nation expressed heartfelt and appropriate emotion and sympathy while simultaneously filling us with hope. Even during dark times, President Reagan pointed to bright days ahead, to the opportunities of the future, to the value of lessons learned through hardship and the necessity of trial to bring forth a triumph.

President Reagan didn't welcome tragedy or hardship, but he did welcome the opportunity to bring hope to the disheartened, direction to the lost, and freedom to the oppressed. That could happen only when facing challenges and making tough, sometimes even unpopular decisions. His overall vision and direction for the country never wavered when crises arose, but he found a way to address each challenge and still stay the course of his overall plan.

In business and in life, anyone can pose as a leader, but only when that person has been tested and proved able to endure hardship will they be classified as a true leader. Anyone can sail a ship through calm, clear waters, but when the seas are stormy, with high waves and eminent peril, only a captain with experience, wisdom, and true leadership can sail through it and bring home a crew—your family members or your employees—that will be stronger, savvier, more seasoned, and better prepared for the next storm. And even the ship—your company or your family—can emerge stronger than when it started. Why? Because the crisis bound everyone together.

Ronald Reagan showed us how we should view crises and how to maximize the lessons and opportunities that challenges bring. How do you view a crisis? As a distraction from or threat to the business at hand? Or as an opportunity to encourage solidarity within your organization and unite everyone behind a common cause? A properly handled crisis or challenge can benefit your overall, long-term profitability and morale even more than extended times of ease and effortless success. Not that crisis and challenge should be desired—absolutely not—but let's face it: Who knows when your company could wind up on the front page of the local paper or on the evening news or unfairly slandered in an online posting unexpectedly. It may be a small incident or one that is tied into an international crisis, or it might even be an internal issue that no one outside the four walls of your company ever knew about that threatens to destroy from within.

A crisis has likely come upon you in some form, and if it hasn't, it probably will. So, like death and taxes, which are inevitable for everyone, how do you prepare yourself to respond to and maximize the inevitable challenges to ultimately work to your advantage?

Ronald Reagan showed us how he accepted both political and personal crises and sought to appropriately address the incidents, always remembering the overall direction he had previously established, rather than allowing the crisis to redirect him. Maintaining parallel themes of hope for the future and optimism for better days ahead, as president, Ronald Reagan instilled confidence in the abilities and commitment of those with whom he had surrounded himself, and as the Great Communicator, he conveyed with confidence to others his vision for the overall direction of his plan. He exuded calmness, even in the midst of a crisis, and empowered those who heard him to also believe in endless possibilities for success ahead.

In business, in politics, and in your personal life there will be a crisis. Even an eternal optimist will reluctantly agree that a challenge will inevitably come your way. It may be a health crisis, family problem, or financial struggle. Regardless of the category or type, a crisis is coming or has already arrived. Although this may sound a bit pessimistic, it is an unwelcome reality. True optimists, however, remember the power they have to overcome a crisis once it does inevitably arrive.

The distinguishing factor between a mediocre leader and an exceptional leader is how a crisis is handled. Does it stop you in your tracks, cripple you emotionally, or cause you to react negatively? True leadership is not always seen in times of ease but often shows itself most clearly when the stakes are high and the pressure is on. How you handle difficult times as a leader is the great differentiator. The risk is greatest when times are challenging, but this is also where the greatest potential for reward and opportunity lies.

In the midst of military conflict, the greatest danger is on the front line, where forces clash to defend, or to seize the most valuable positions on the battlefield. So that is where commanders put their strongest forces—in the areas where the crisis is the most dire. Militarily, the strongest forces would not be sent to protect or capture areas where there are few resources or worthless assets.

Similarly, in business, if you are not investing in the areas of your business that are particularly challenging, competitive, or controversial, you may perhaps be missing the greatest areas of potential growth and profitability for your company. Of course, you don't want to knowingly walk your business into situations that will create a crisis, but you should consider that your greatest leadership opportunities may come in the midst of a challenge on the front lines.

Crisis = Danger + Opportunity

No arsenal or no weapon in the arsenals of the world is so formidable as the will and moral courage of free men and women.

—Ronald Reagan[*]

Whether dealing with a crisis in your business or within your family, there is always an element of danger and an element of opportunity. A real leader needs to see beyond the impulsive panic of the moment and look for the primary danger of the crisis and minimize it, as well as identify the primary opportunity and maximize it. Rather than giving in to the moment of the crisis by yelling, screaming, or overreacting, a true leader steps back and identifies the primary danger and develops a way to minimize it. A true leader also identifies the primary opportunity within the crisis and looks for ways to maximize it, driving everyone and everything positively forward. Although it is usually fairly easy to identify a long list of dangers, with some thought and creativity there is always at least one opportunity to be found and pursued as well.

In talking with a friend who is the CEO of his family business, this crisis = danger + opportunity scenario was clearly displayed. Due to consistent and complete negligence on the part of my friend's brother-in-law, it was evident that my friend was going to have to fire him. As we talked about his personal internal struggle in the midst of this professional crisis, I helped him talk through both the dangers and the opportunities for him and for

---

[*]*Source:* First Inaugural Address, January 20, 1981.

his company in the midst of this very challenging and very personal crisis.

He identified the dangers easily: Firing his brother-in-law could jeopardize his personal relationship with both his sister and his brother-in-law. It could split the family and alienate family members who didn't fully understand the situation. It could divide his family into sides and ultimately sever relationships that were valuable and meaningful to him.

The opportunities were more difficult for him to initially find, but once he began to articulate them, it became apparent that he was making the right decision. It would give him the opportunity to prove that the best interests of the company came first, that insubordination would not be tolerated, and that laziness, negligence, and lack of interest would not be rewarded, regardless of the personal relationship.

By demonstrating true leadership through ultimately firing his brother-in-law, he earned great respect from his other employees. They knew that the stakes for him were personally very high, which made a powerful statement professionally. As a result of his willingness to justifiably fire his own brother-in-law, the rest of his employees were motivated to work harder, convinced that they were being watched and were being held to a high standard. Even more important, they felt their work was genuinely valued and needed, because my friend proved he was the kind of person who would only surround himself with creative, talented, hardworking people.

The employees of course had been watching the brother-in-law's lack of effort for years. Because senior leadership had previously ignored his lack of commitment to the job and to the company, other employees assumed that loyalty and dedication weren't valued or required. My friend's decision to fire his own brother-in-law silently spoke volumes about his priorities and vision for the company and about his commitment to pursue that vision, regardless of the personal ramifications.

Ultimately, the brother-in-law, who earlier had felt obligated to participate in the family business, was free to pursue a career that he was passionate about and where he felt fulfilled. A crisis had been faced head-on, and the results were rewarding and beneficial for everyone involved.

So how do you handle a crisis? Are you vindictive, vengeful, bitter, and irrational, or is your response calm, reasonable, level headed, and professional? Others will emulate you, for better or for worse. Navigating crises by focusing on the opportunity, not exclusively on the danger, you can help others learn to accept and appropriately manage crises in their own lives as well.

Even in the midst of personal crisis this same model applies. Another friend of mine recently found out his wife had just filed for divorce—a complete shock to him. He feared losing everything—his wife, his kids, his house, and his whole life—all legitimate dangers. When I encouraged him to look for the opportunities and maximize them, he was convinced there weren't any. I pressed him to think of some opportunities, and he said that he was hoping to get this behind him quickly and ultimately find someone else who loved him—both real opportunities.

I said, "But what is the *real* opportunity? It's staring you right in the face." He adamantly believed there wasn't one.

"I don't see it," he said.

I continued, "Your kids are watching. Your employees are watching. Your family is watching to see how you handle this crisis. They will emulate in their own lives how to handle this crisis by watching you. So are you going to lead?"

And his response was so incredible. He said, "Oh my gosh—I've been a mess."

And I responded back to him, "And no one would blame you for that. But that can change today."

And he said, "Oh, it will change today." And it did.

Now when I see him, he says to me, "I'm in a crisis. Danger—minimize, opportunity—maximize, and drive myself and everyone toward it." And then he smiles.

You too have the power to completely transform, right here, right now, the way you view crises for the rest of your life. To view them for what they are, and to sift through the rubbish and find the opportunities waiting there.

A leader is always watched. A true leader realizes this and is consistently professional and proactive in their decision making and pursues excellence, *especially* in the midst of a crisis!

Focus on the Opening

We in government should learn to look at our country with the eyes of the entrepreneur, seeing possibilities where others see only problems.

—Ronald Reagan[*]

Maintaining your focus on the bigger picture is an integral part of crisis management. Picture yourself as a NASCAR driver, racing down the track. A crash occurs directly in front of you.

[*]*Source:* Radio Address to the Nation on Economic Growth, January 26, 1985.

Picture a cloud of debris with one clear opening in the middle. Where will your focus be? Where should your focus be?

Where your focus goes is where you will go, as will the team that follows you. Will you focus on and steer right into the debris and wind up off the track? Or worse?

Are you focused on the opening in front of you? Or on the debris flying all around you?

Will you miraculously appear unscathed on the other side of that cloud of smoke because you kept your eyes steadily on the opening?

What appropriate symbolism for business and life. We often focus on the debris—the negative and the challenges, wondering if there is any way out. Instead, we need to focus on the opportunities that still exist around us, on the productive aspects of our business that fit within our vision and will move us successfully forward, past, and through the debris.

As you implement your own plan of action to reach your visionary goals, you also will face adversity. You'll face challenges, hurdles, and crises. Do not be surprised when you do, just plan now to face crisis with positive action and realistic optimism.

Overcoming Distractions

We will always remember. We will always be proud. We will always be prepared, so we may always be free.

—Ronald Reagan[*]

---

[*]*Source:* Remarks Commemorating the 40th Anniversary of the Normandy Invasion, June 6, 1984.

We associate the 1980s with the expansion of personal liberty and political freedom abroad and the ending of the Cold War. How interesting, because those are the two main areas to which Ronald Reagan initially turned his presidency's focus and addressed. How success is measured within each of those areas is perhaps subjective, but there is no doubting that Ronald Reagan accomplished the communication of a clear vision as president and took great strides toward achievement.

Yet clearly outlining and then achieving his goals was not nearly as simple as hindsight might make it appear. As in every decade prior, America in the 1980s did not exist in isolation and had to be simultaneously proactive on the world stage and reactive to events that happened both within and beyond our borders, beyond our control, and yet still affected our nation and its people.

During the Reagan presidency there was an economic crisis in Europe; widespread famine in Africa; continued unrest, violence, and war throughout the Middle East; and political upheaval in Poland, Hungary, Romania, and Czechoslovakia. In Asia, struggles continued in Vietnam, Cambodia, the Philippines, and China. There were wars, coups, and uprisings in Iraq, Iran, Argentina, the Falkland Islands, Lebanon, and Grenada, among others.

Amid all of these competing challenges, crises, and cries for humanitarian aid, political involvement, and military force, President Reagan remained resolute, appropriately responding only when and how it fit within his overall goals and vision for America to do so. He also chose carefully when not to involve the United States—or to limit U.S. involvement. Ronald Reagan again provides a great example to follow, selectively and strategically choosing a posture or pursuit, rather than allowing others to dictate or define your role or response as a leader.

Whenever my son, Justin, thinks there is any chance he might get in trouble, he falls back on an old joke. He points into the distance and says, "Look, a distraction!" and tries to change the subject from a potential punishment. We all laugh, of course, but maybe he is on to something. Life is busy with lots of competition for your time, distractions from your goals, and pressures and activities vying for energy and attention. As a leader, you need to control, direct, and prioritize those competing interests and maintain your previously determined course.

One of my biggest frustrations with CEOs, especially friends of mine who run organizations or companies, is that they want to go from point A to point B, and two years later they end up at point M with no idea how they got there or what happened to their original plan. They get thrown off course because they allow themselves to. When adversity comes their way, they abandon their plan, divert all of their energy and attention to address the current challenge, and lose track of where they were and what they were doing before the distraction arose. They completely lose sight of their original vision and don't even realize it.

Ron Bailey, a board member of one of my companies, always gives me sound advice. One day while we were discussing the future of my title company, I said, "I think I'm going to start a mortgage company to feed my title business." There was a moment of silence, and Ron said, "Interesting, Dan. I thought you were in the title business. Maybe you should just do that and do it really well." In the end I will ultimately make the final decision, but remember that I always listen, and listen carefully, to my Kitchen Cabinet. After much thought, I decided to stay focused exclusively on the title business and was much better off because of it.

In business it is easy to be tempted and distracted by elements of your projects that may only be loosely related, or even unnecessary, for advancing your overall vision. You could spend days or weeks crafting the perfect slogan for a new product, but that may not currently be the most critical piece of your overall success.

Ronald Reagan found many opportunities to simply repeat his vision, as many times as possible to as many people as possible. Using speeches, fireside chats, and other public forums, President Reagan constantly reminded the American people—and the world—of his goals.

Repetition of your vision reminds you what you have really set out to do, helps with ongoing evaluation of what is truly important to accomplish, and avoids diversion by distractions. Are you focusing too much on the bells and whistles, or on details that may or may not become important later? If your repetition of the vision doesn't match your current actions, you need to stop and refocus. Keep your eyes on what is really important, and plan accordingly. You'll accomplish much more, and eventually will wind up where you intend to go and not fall prey to needless distractions.

Reiterating the vision to people around you, such as family, colleagues, and friends, will help keep them connected to your goals, even if those people are unrelated to your goal. Outside perspectives can motivate you, keeping you focused on your key priorities and objectives. When people know what you are doing, they'll check up on you and ask about your progress. Some may help you in small or big ways that can become a critical component to your overall success and ultimate achievement.

When you have 20 goals, you will see lots of activity, but very little accomplishment. Your distractions will be many, and likely only a few of your objectives will ever successfully be completed because you will jump from task to task, conflicted over what should receive priority or primary attention. Prioritize and allocate appropriately to match your overall goals and vision, which will allow you to make meaningful progress.

Competition Creates Opportunity

Excellence demands competition. . . . Without a race there can be no champion, no records broken, no excellence.

—Ronald Reagan[*]

Competition is the most recognized form of challenge or adversity in business. It is what free markets are based on, and to succeed, you need to give your business the strongest advantage over your competitors. Although it may be a bit counterintuitive, this usually means striving to be better than your competition in only a couple of strategically selected goals rather than attempting to be better than others at everything. Think about where you have the advantage. If you're the smaller player, don't fight on price; become known for something else, such as your exceptional, personalized customer service.

You will need to evaluate the resources you have and strategically analyzed how best to use them to promote your strengths.

---

[*]*Source:* Remarks to the National Catholic Education Association in Chicago, Illinois, April 15, 1982.

With today's social media and instant communication, lots of tools are available to you. Creativity goes a long way toward expanding the effectiveness of your efforts and earning media and attention, not just paying for it.

In the end, what matters most is the implementation of the plan. A leader's most crucial role is to keep everyone focused on the vision and the tasks involved in bringing it to life. Revisit the vision every day, talk regularly to those involved in executing the elements of the plan, and keep everyone focused, engaged, motivated, and enthusiastic about reaching the end goal. Some businesses try to overcome competition by covering every base, analyzing all of the elements of their market and attempting to be a well-rounded company. Although that may sound logical, the problem with being a jack-of-all-trades is that you become a master of none. There is no arena in which you stand out, and no service you can point to and say, "I am the best in the industry at that." It is wise to seek to improve the area of your business that is the weakest, but always remember your strengths as well. Use those strengths to gain and retain a competitive edge in your market.

Competition requires resources, and they will always be limited. Ronald Reagan was able to harness the economic power of the United States and focus resources on developing the Strategic Defense Initiative, a ground- and space-based defense system. Although the United States made significant strides pursuing new technology, just the threat of jumping ahead of Soviet military capabilities was enough to get them to the negotiating table and help them realize that *glasnost* and *perestroika*, or openness and reform, were the only feasible options for the future of the Soviet Union.

Although President Reagan faced many competing challenges domestically, including battling to revive the nation's economy, internationally he called out Communism as his greatest foe. Notice that he was not competing with the Soviet people or even directly with their leaders; he defined the competition as democracy versus Communism. Clear, effective, ambitious. As Ronald Reagan demonstrated, one of the first steps to overcoming competition is to make sure the foe is properly identified and the vision for victory is clearly outlined and articulated.

In business you will have the same challenges. Although the easy answer to the "Who is your competition?" question is usually the number one or number two leader in your industry, you may have greater success focusing elsewhere. Consider that sometimes your closest competition might be a substitute product or variation on your product or just overcoming the lack of awareness of your product or company—in which case you are your own worst competition.

Think through all the things that are preventing or slowing your growth, and you'll have a good starting point. Now narrow the list to two to three items that could make the biggest difference toward expanding and growing your company, looking for the opportunities that exist within a competitive environment.

Overcoming Setbacks

The future doesn't belong to the fainthearted; it belongs to the brave.

—Ronald Reagan[*]

_____

[*]*Source:* Address to the Nation following the explosion of the Space Shuttle *Challenger*, January 28, 1986.

America was founded by brave and rugged individuals seeking personal liberty and the freedom to choose their own destiny. Likewise, the American West was explored and settled by those who wished for more—more land, more independence, more gold, more self-determination. Driven by curiosity, a spirit of adventure, and the lure of the great unknown, brave explorers settled America despite great risk, yet they willingly faced that risk for the hope of even greater reward.

In the business frontier, brave entrepreneurs continually try to build, create, and expand into new areas of discovery, technology, or innovation. They do so at great personal risk and often personal expense to push the boundaries of design, purpose, or product just a bit further than has ever been done before. They do so knowing they cannot have rewards without taking risks, and they willingly, and boldly press forward anyway.

In Charles Koch's book *The Science of Success*, I admired the inclusion of a list of all the successful companies and industries which they built or in which they have been invested—and appreciated even more the inclusion of a list of the companies they started that failed. Charles Koch, and his brother, David, are extremely successful and have seen their share of rewards. Yet they realize, as all good leaders do, that success does not come without also assuming, managing, and bravely facing risk.

With risk inevitably comes failure at times. A great leader handles success with humility and caution, appropriately acknowledges failure, and then presses forward again with inspiration and determination toward the visionary goal ahead. Setbacks will certainly come, so how can you as a leader prepare to perpetuate and advance your vision while still properly addressing them?

There is no clearer example of addressing setbacks appropriately than Ronald Reagan's response following the Space Shuttle *Challenger* disaster on January 28, 1986, when tragedy struck the skies above Kennedy Space Center. Just 73 seconds into its flight, the *Challenger* broke apart in the sky, leading to the deaths of its seven crew members.

Due to the presence on board of Christa McAuliffe, the first teacher going to space, many viewed the launch live, including schoolchildren all across the nation. I remember vividly watching the launch from my classroom and seeing the horrific images on the television. I could not truly comprehend what had happened, but I knew it was tragic and devastating. I was shocked, saddened, and speechless.

Later that same evening, I watched as a very solemn, very sincere President Reagan gave a speech that would speak to and on behalf of a nation in sorrow—and begin the process of healing.

He immediately addressed the tragedy. He sincerely conveyed the grief he felt within his own heart, which was shared across the nation, but he didn't abandon us in our mourning or let us linger without hope. He respectfully lifted our thoughts beyond the immediate sorrows and renewed the country's dedication to the Space Shuttle program with the following excerpted remarks.

> *Today is a day for mourning and remembering. Nancy and I are pained to the core by the tragedy of the shuttle* Challenger. *We know we share this pain with all of the people of our country. This is truly a national loss. For the families of the seven, we cannot bear, as you do, the full impact of this tragedy. But we feel the loss, and we're thinking about you so very much. Your loved ones were daring and brave, and they had that special grace, that special spirit that says, "Give me a challenge and I'll meet it with joy."*

They had a hunger to explore the universe and discover its truths. They wished to serve, and they did. They served all of us.

And I want to say something to the schoolchildren of America who were watching the live coverage of the shuttle's takeoff. I know it's hard to understand, but sometimes painful things like this happen. It's all part of the process of exploration and discovery. It's all part of taking a chance and expanding man's horizons. The future doesn't belong to the fainthearted; it belongs to the brave. The Challenger *crew was pulling us into the future, and we'll continue to follow them. . . . Nothing ends here; our hopes and our journeys continue.*

The crew of the space shuttle Challenger *honored us by the manner in which they lived their lives. We will never forget them, nor the last time we saw them, this morning, as they prepared for their journey and waved goodbye and "slipped the surly bonds of earth" to "touch the face of God."*

—Ronald Reagan, January 28, 1986

At the moment of the *Challenger* disaster, President Reagan acknowledged the nation's horror and pain, while at the same time keeping its faith in NASA, our space program, and in America's strength. The absolute worst result from a setback, no matter how large or small, is people losing faith and giving up. President Reagan took great care to thank and honor the *Challenger* crew for their dedication, bravery, and sacrifice and to make sure the families of the crew knew that all of America had them in their thoughts and prayers.

In that speech, he didn't point fingers or call out people for failures. It was not needed and was not appropriate at that time. The disaster had taken lives away from loving families, but President Reagan would not let it take away America's faith in its space program. He overcame adversity and setbacks by acknowledging the emotions that were evident and strong and gave continued hope and vision for the future without wavering.

That was authentic, genuine leadership—and a true example of inspirational leadership as well. He acknowledged the pain, yet brought us all to a better place, which was forward looking and hopeful. We, as leaders, have the chance to do the same thing with those around us by recognizing their hurt or loss or worry, but also challenging them to rise above and look forward, and believe that nothing ends here.

Although I didn't think it was possible to hold Ronald Reagan in higher esteem, it happened that day. Not only because I liked him personally or agreed with him politically, but, on that day, he earned my trust and the trust of a nation seeking strength to lean on and renewed hope for a bright future.

And shouldn't trust be at the very core of leadership? Trust that the needs of the group will outweigh the personal needs of the leader. Trust that the goals for long-term overall progress will predicate any short-term political agenda. In the midst of a space shuttle mission tragedy, Ronald Reagan's leadership mission was accomplished and appreciated. He was sincere, trusted, and genuine. He was leadership personified.

Adjusting Course

I do not believe in a fate that will fall on us no matter what we do. I do believe in a fate that will fall on us if we do nothing.

—Ronald Reagan[*]

---

[*]*Source:* First Inaugural address, Washington, D. C., January 20, 1981.

Of course, the future is not a fixed point, and many factors and variables are in constant motion that can help, or hinder, attainment of your goals. Even in the most carefully constructed plans there are no absolutes or guarantees. Flexibility and adaptability—essentially the ability to grow and change, sometimes painfully—must be woven into the fabric of your personal life and into your company or organization. When there's no room for change, there is no room for growth. But don't let a changing landscape discourage you or become an excuse for mediocrity or laziness. Your competition will adjust, forcing you to adjust, too.

Sometimes in personal or professional relationships, two sides can begin squabbling over their respective interests or areas of disagreement. Rather than allowing the frustration and tension to build, the approach can be changed by stopping the conversation and saying, "Let's start again." Then restart by first covering areas where the two sides can agree.

In business you need to look for similar windows of opportunity. If part of your plan isn't working, instead of instinctively doubling down, you may want to consider pulling back and finding a different approach that may be more effective.

Overcoming Apathy

It is time for us to realize that we're too great a nation to limit ourselves to small dreams.

—Ronald Reagan[*]

---

[*]*Source:* First Inaugural Address, Washington, D. C., January 20, 1981.

Apathy settles in when people disengage from the vision. They may feel like they are spinning their wheels without making progress or that their contribution to the company's vision is not significant or necessary. Apathy is a type of adversity that cuts your support out from underneath you. If it is not addressed, it can leave you as the lonely leader of an army of none.

When President Reagan first took office, he faced a nation that in many ways had given up on being able to transform itself. People had become accustomed to high inflation and unemployment. They hated it, but because past policies had failed to fix the situation, they had become apathetic, skeptical, and disengaged. They had little confidence that the future would bring the change they desired, so they set their hopes low to avoid continued disappointment.

Then along came an optimistic, visionary leader who painted a new picture of possibility. Words mattered in getting everyone reengaged, and inspired them that the future could, and would, be different than the past. This mind-set was essential for recruiting support for and active participants in the new vision and expansive future of America and overcoming the widespread apathy that existed.

As a leader, you need to find ways to help those within your sphere of influence be successful, too. Find ways to encourage people to develop new ideas and take initiative. It is difficult for people to be apathetic about implementing their own ideas, so cultivate the free exchange of ideas between employees and then reward their creativity and initiative as appropriate.

Open the doors for candid communication and take time to strengthen commitment to the overall vision. Don't just repeat the vision like a mantra; although helpful to overcome distraction, this does not combat apathy in the same way. If people are feeling apathetic, it means the vision has lost meaning to them. Simply saying the same words over and over again likely will not bring them back on board. Fighting apathy means explaining and articulating the vision so that everyone understands how the vision relates to them, how they contribute to its realization, and what the benefits are of attaining the vision that has been outlined.

Look for leaders and champions of your vision throughout your organizational structure. Future leaders can often be identified by the way they contribute to the advancement of overall goals and vision, regardless of their position or title. Overcoming apathy can be as simple as rewarding success, and praising creative, productive effort, lessening restrictions, and unleashing creativity and enthusiasm.

★ ★ ★

Handling Crisis

Strive to be a better leader by modeling better decision making when the dangers are the greatest. Because in the end, the difference between mediocre leadership and exceptional leadership is the way you handle a crisis—finding opportunity in every challenge. Ronald Reagan truly believed that "It CAN Be Done"—both in times of ease and in times of conflict. Your goal as a leader is to identify and minimize the danger, identify and maximize the opportunity, and drive you and everyone else toward it. This life changing revelation will forever allow you to view crises differently.

Realize that when a crisis does come your way, everyone is watching to see how you will handle it. It is a chance for you to truly embody leadership excellence, realizing that everyone from your family, your friends, and your coworkers may emulate your actions and attitude in their own lives. Ultimately a crisis, and those going through it, are bound together by the challenge and have the opportunity to come out the other side of it even stronger than they started.

To do so, you have to focus on the opening in front of you, not the debris flying all around you. It is so easy to get caught up in negativity and the distractions of life, but if we are willing to commit to competitive greatness, to work smarter, but not necessarily harder, to overcome setbacks, and ultimately to show inspirational leadership, bringing people to a better place, then we have a chance for greater success. We may have to adjust course along the way, or overcome apathy, which is human nature, but that's where the leadership opportunity truly exists.

As we struggle to face the obstacles that arise each day, the successes we have had in overcoming past challenges often fade from memory. We would be wise to not only survive our challenges but learn to thrive in them; we should recognize the strategies of success that previously moved us forward and remember to apply them in future crises, realizing that the greatest opportunities can result from overcoming a crisis with character and conviction.

How exciting it is to be able to accept your role as someone who can inspire, communicate, and motivate others to be the best that they can be. When you accept this challenge, you are closer to being able to *Lead Like Reagan.*

7 Changing the World

Leaving a Lasting Legacy

Some may tell us that this is the end of an era. But what they overlook is that in America, every day is a new beginning, and every sunset is merely the latest milestone on a voyage that never ends. For this is the land that has never become, but is always in the act of becoming.

—Ronald Reagan[*]

---

[*]*Source:* Presidential Medal of Freedom Ceremony at the White House, January 13, 1993.

*L*ead Like Reagan is successfully achieved day in and day out in the trenches of life and business. Although each small step or decision along the way may not be remembered or seem monumental, when you look back upon the combined power and force of countless decisions, that is where you will find the evidence and the impact of your cumulative leadership.

Though you should not lead by looking back with regret or longing to events of the past, you should still learn from them, grow from them, and glean the elements of success from them. That said, you should not live in the future either, consumed with worry about what your legacy will be. You must live in the present, cherishing each and every moment. Yet it may be beneficial to pause periodically and think about how you will be remembered when you are no longer around. What will they remember about how you lived? About how you led? Is that the legacy you want to leave? If not, start today to lead—and live—in a way that will create the legacy of leadership that you desire.

In a post–presidential address on May 15, 1993, Ronald Reagan made the following remarks at the Citadel Commencement in Charleston, South Carolina. Far from political in tone, his speech challenged the audience to invest in the development of their character in addition to the acquisition and application of knowledge. Wise words indeed.

Sometimes, you see, life gives us what we think is fair warning of the choices that will shape our future. On such occasions we are able to look far along the path, up ahead to that distant point in the woods where the poet's two roads diverge. And then, if we are wise, we will take time to think and reflect before choosing which road to take before the junction is reached.

But such occasions, in fact, are rather rare. Far more often than we can comfortably admit, the most crucial of life's moments come like the scriptural "thief in the night." Suddenly and without notice, the crisis is upon us and the moment of choice is at hand— a moment fraught with import for ourselves, and for all who are depending on the choice we make. We find ourselves, if you will, plunged without warning into the icy water, where the currents of moral consequence run swift and deep, and where our fellow man and yes, I believe, our Maker are waiting to see whether we will pass the rope.

These are the moments when instinct and character take command, for there is no time, at such moments, for anything but fortitude and integrity. Debate and reflection and a leisurely weighing of the alternatives are luxuries we do not have. The only question is what kind of responsibility will come to the fore.

And now we come to the heart of the matter, to the core lesson taught by heroism, for, you see, the character that takes command in moments of crucial choices has already been determined.

It has been determined by a thousand other choices made earlier in seemingly unimportant moments. It has been determined by all the little choices of years past—by all those times when the voice of conscience was at war with the voice of temptation— whispering the lie that it really doesn't matter.

It has been determined by all the day-to-day decisions made when life seemed easy and crises seemed far away—the decision that, piece by piece, bit by bit, developed habits of discipline or of laziness; habits of self-sacrifice or self-indulgence; habits of duty and honor and integrity—or dishonor and shame.

Because when life does get tough, and the crisis is undeniably at hand—when we must, in an instant, look inward for strength of character to see us through—we will find nothing inside ourselves that we have not already put there.

Lead Like Reagan

Freedom is a fragile thing and is never more than one generation away from extinction. It is not ours by inheritance; it must be fought for and defended constantly by each generation, for it comes only once to a people. Those who have known freedom, then lost it, have never known it again.

—Ronald Reagan[*]

It is difficult to top two presidential terms as monumental and transformative as Ronald Reagan's. He left office with the highest approval rating of any departing president and a lasting imprint of expanded freedom on the nation and the world. As he did so, he looked back with humility at all that had been accomplished—sharing his successes with those who had helped him achieve them—and with those who had elected him as their president. In his farewell address to the nation from the Oval Office, he ends by saying:

We've done our part. And as I walk off into the city streets, a final word to the men and women of the Reagan Revolution, the men and women across America who for eight years did the work that brought America back. My friends: We did it. We weren't just marking time. We made a difference. We made the city stronger; we made the city freer; and we left her in good hands. All in all, not bad—not bad at all.

---

[*] *Source:* First Inaugural Address as the 33rd Governor of California, January 5, 1967.

When you retire from your company, or ultimately depart from this world, will you look back and confidently say that you did your part, that you didn't just mark time, and made a difference? Will you have made everything around you stronger and freer and left your family, your organization, your community, and the world around you in good hands? I hope so!

Even though many dramatic changes like the fall of the Berlin Wall didn't happen until after President Reagan left office, the optimistic momentum that he had fostered toward that end was unstoppable. The speed with which events unfolded may have surprised even President Reagan, although he never doubted the outcome.

Similarly, America's recovery brought the country back to a position of respect in the world. Other Western-style economies around the globe replicated our economic miracle with similar results. Maybe in the most powerful testament to Reagan's vision, even the Soviet Union and Communist China started discussing and experimenting with some Reagan-like economic policies.

President Reagan had accomplished the two goals he had articulated to the American people, and his influence on history was just starting. The impact of his life and leadership was lasting. Now that's a legacy!

Invest in Others

Some people wonder all their lives if they've made a difference. The Marines don't have that problem.

—Ronald Reagan[*]

---

[*]*Source:* From a personal letter written to Lance Corporal Joe Hickey, September 23, 1983.

For security reasons, President Reagan often had to enter
or leave an event through a loading dock entrance, back door,
empty hallway, or busy kitchen. During these private times
behind the scenes when no cameras were rolling, many
observed that these were some of President Reagan's most
shining and memorable moments. If the schedule left even
just a few seconds of time to spare, he would regularly stop
to shake hands, look into the eyes of the people who were
helping and participating in the event, and genuinely thank
ordinary Americans for their hard work. This is real leadership—and why he is remembered as he is. This is who he
was when no one was watching. Those few who observed his
simple, ordinary kindness and extraordinary humility were
changed—and inspired.

Although the way in which he treated people was basically
common courtesy, for someone in his position it was noticed,
admired, and appreciated because it was very contrary to the
behavior of a typical bossy, demanding leader. Who knows
what inspiration some of these individuals recall from their
short interactions with the president of the United States?
Most were likely surprised that he noticed them at all and
then took the time to acknowledge them. I guarantee that
small action made a huge and lasting impact on those
individuals. Hopefully they have chosen to emulate those
traits of great leadership in their own lives, knowing the
effect of simple acts of civility.

President Reagan firmly believed and demonstrated daily
his belief that everyone is important. He treated even his
greatest political adversaries with dignity and respect and
accomplished much, much more than he would have if he

had consistently attacked them. He also had a lasting and positive effect on those who disagreed with him, making them more likely to compromise with him in the future and think favorably of him, even if they held different beliefs.

Following Ronald Reagan's example, I have always made an effort to thank and engage people I meet along the way. Over time, I've learned valuable information about a company's culture or the local communities, which has helped me personalize a speech or close a sale. I give 100 percent of myself in all my presentations, but occasionally wonder, and even hope, if some of my one-on-one conversations with people before and after a speech have a bigger impact than my actual formal presentations themselves.

There's a temptation to focus on the perceived task at hand exclusively, while sometimes an equal, or perhaps even greater, opportunity lies through awareness of the people and circumstance around you and your choice to proactively interact favorably and positively with them.

Although it is crucial to get the "big things" right when it comes to your leadership, your legacy will not necessarily be remembered by your mission statement, corporate vision, or personal goals. Instead it will be remembered by the little things you did for people—or to people—along the way. Unfortunately, one poor interaction can undo many of your longtime leadership efforts. However, the good news is that just one positive interaction can do the exact opposite and leave a favorable and lasting impression on others. So take advantage of those little moments and do big things! It's an investment in others that will ultimately impact your own legacy.

The Power of Gratitude

It's been the honor of my life to be your president. So many of you have written the past few weeks to say thanks, but I could say as much for you. Nancy and I are grateful for the opportunity you gave us to serve.

—Ronald Reagan[*]

President Reagan made a personal connection with people. I was blessed to be able to watch time and time again the impact he had on others and how he inspired them to do and be their best. In his post–presidency years in Los Angeles, Ronald Reagan's car arrived at the office at almost the exact same time every morning. He was a man of discipline, keeping a busy schedule well into his 80s (again, a powerful example of his commitment to principles and to people, rather than committing to his own leisure or personal pursuits—even in his twilight years!). As the president arrived at the office every morning, the building's doorman would run ahead to hold open the door for him. The doorman had purchased an American flag, which he would hold in one hand as he held the door in the other hand for the president each day.

One day as he was driving in, President Reagan called and asked me to meet him downstairs with some presidential gifts from the gift closet. I grabbed some pens, a tie tack, and cufflinks, all beautifully boxed and wrapped and embossed with the presidential seal. As I met the president at the curb, he motioned for me to come over; he had a childlike look in his eyes, excited to surprise the doorman. He took the gifts, exited the car, and walked straight to the doorman, who was starting to shake

---

[*]*Source:* Farewell Address to the Nation, January 11, 1989.

nervously as the president approached him, rather than walking past him as usual.

Ronald Reagan stopped, looked this man in the eye, and thanked him for his excellence and hard work each and every day, for the obvious pride he took in his job, and for his thoughtfulness and respect in buying and holding an American flag.

President Reagan said, "Thank you for what you do every day—which is make my day!" He then reached over to shake the doorman's hand and give him the gifts—but by this time, the man was shaking, trying to hold the door and the flag, shake hands, take the gifts, and couldn't do it all. He was overwhelmed by Ronald Reagan's kindness and thoughtful awareness, and I was a wide-eyed young man who was taking it all in, watching real leadership up close and at the highest level. What an impact it made on me—for life!

We all know the effect of a simple, thoughtful gift—or even the power of a basic handwritten thank-you note. We know the meaning behind them because we all can personally recall when we received something particularly poignant and touching. So if you know how these acts of kindness have affected you, I have to ask—are you doing any? Do you have the discipline to always send a thank-you note to follow up with people you meet? Or do you take the time and forethought to arrive at a meeting with a small token that says, "This is important to me—and *you* and your time are important to me." Your small habits today are a big part of your lasting impact.

Focus on What Matters

You and I have a rendezvous with destiny. We will preserve for our children this, the last best hope of man on earth, or we will sentence them to take the first step into a thousand years of darkness. If we fail, at least let our children and our children's children say of us we justified our brief moment here. We did all that could be done.

—Ronald Reagan[*]

Perhaps your faith plays a role in defining for you what is lasting and what truly matters. Politically, there may also be essential elements of your belief system that are important to you to pass along. Personally, there are little ways to create a big and lasting impact, and professionally your legacy needs to be considered and cultivated as well; take care to lead and live with excellence worthy of emulation.

In President Reagan's case, after leaving office, he was able to build on the tradition of establishing a presidential library. Many presidential libraries house a collection of the president's writings, photos, memorabilia, and mementos from their life and time in office and include a small museum.

Ronald Reagan personally wanted to ensure that the Ronald Reagan Presidential Foundation and Library in Simi Valley, California, was also dedicated to ongoing education and learning—and would use its vast resources and knowledge base to inform and empower others, primarily the next generation of leaders. The Reagan Library is as lively, interactive, memorable, and inspiring as the man whose name it bears. It has a beautifully renovated interactive museum dedicated to Ronald Reagan's life and presidency, including underground vaults containing photographs and historic papers.

[*]*Source:* "A Time for Choosing" speech, October 27, 1964.

One area is reserved for research scholars, and a Discovery Center allows students to reenact an international crisis, participating as either a member of the White House press corps, the U.S. military, or the executive branch of the government. The Reagan Library also has the retired Air Force One airplane, which served five presidents. It also has the Reagan Pub, a bar moved all the way to Simi Valley, California, from Ballyporeen, Ireland, where Ronald Reagan's ancestors once lived.

The library regularly hosts public policy forums where thought leaders of the day engage their audiences in substantive ways, reflecting on the impact of the Reagan legacy with gratitude but also looking forward to the ways in which the lessons of the past can be applied with success to the future. Through programs such as this, the Ronald Reagan Presidential Foundation and Library continues to be relevant and is consistently engaged with the issues of the day. It is a living, thriving entity that continues to grow and change, rather than existing as a stagnant remembrance of the past.

What a great analogy for our lives as well. Do we look to rest on the laurels of our past? Or do we want to continue to grow, learn, and develop ourselves, expanding our influence, importance, and ultimately our impact? Focusing on things that are greater than ourselves and that have significance will help ensure that we are focusing on that which truly matters and will be lasting and meaningful.

Since my desire is to constantly promote the legacy of Ronald Reagan and share the impact of his life upon me, my business partner Peggy Grande, who also worked closely with the president, and I have created an executive leadership training program for business leaders using the leadership traits of Ronald

Reagan in a nonpolitical way. We host these programs at the Reagan Library, which provides an outstanding location for inspiration, making a profound and lasting impact on those who attend. The Reagan Experience helps companies and individuals learn how to create a vision, build a team, communicate their message, take action and manage crisis.

I'm particularly proud of my long association with the Ronald Reagan Presidential Foundation and Library in Simi Valley, California. If you have not had the opportunity to visit the Reagan Library, I would highly recommend you do so. I am confident that your visit will be both meaningful and memorable.

Inspire Optimism

We Americans have never been pessimists. We conquer fear with faith, and we overwhelm threats and hardship with courage, work, opportunity, and freedom.

—Ronald Reagan[*]

Many citizens of former Eastern Bloc countries attribute their freedom to President Reagan's leadership on the world stage. He didn't go to war with the Soviet Union; he simply inspired optimism in the Soviet people and in oppressed people worldwide. It was the citizens of those countries who ultimately rose up and chose freedom and liberty over tyranny. They had needed—and received in President Reagan—a road map for freedom and the inspiration to pursue it.

---

[*]*Source:* Radio Address to the Nation on Economic Recovery and National Defense, December 18, 1982.

I will always remember a frail, elderly Romanian woman coming into the post–presidency Office of Ronald Reagan for a brief visit. She literally fell to the president's feet, overwhelmed with emotion, sobbing and kissing his feet and thanking him for freeing her, freeing her family, and freeing her people from oppression. Talk about having an impact! Although our decisions and actions may not topple Communism or free entire nations, we can have a memorable and lasting impact on others and positively inspire them and change the course of their lives.

When you inspire someone, they capture your vision and make it their own. When you inspire someone, you don't need to threaten or force them into action—they freely engage—and do so with passion and energy. What you do affects others. You can choose to be deathly toxic or positively contagious. I make a conscious effort to choose positively contagious every time. So given the same two choices, which will you choose? What kind of leader will you be?

Your Life Legacy

I know in my heart that man is good. That what is right will always eventually triumph. And there's purpose and worth to each and every life.

—Ronald Reagan[*]
(Inscription on Ronald Reagan's Memorial Site)

Ronald Reagan's lasting impact was never clearer than on Saturday, June 5, 2004, when at the age of 93, he passed away.

---

[*]*Source:* Remarks at the Ronald Reagan Presidential Library Dedication, Simi Valley, CA, November 4, 1991.

Following his death, if you looked at the outpouring from every corner of this country—and from around the world—of affection and respect for a man whom many never even met, you realized that this man affected people in a way unlike any other modern leader. People felt a connection with him, as he had with them.

Like Ronald Reagan, we all want to believe that "America's best days are yet ahead," but after President Reagan's passing, President George Bush appropriately remarked, "With the passing of Ronald Reagan, some of America's best days are behind us—and that is worth our tears." His was a life with lasting impact and meaningful legacy.

For me personally, on the day President Reagan passed away, I received a phone call from Peggy Grande, President Reagan's personal assistant for 10 years. She told me the news and asked me, "What are you doing this week?"

I replied, "Anything you need me to do."

"Can you be on a plane to California today?"

"Of course." So I flew to Los Angeles that day and was honored to play a role in implementing the plan for President Reagan's interment service at the Reagan Library in Simi Valley, California.

As we worked through the events of the week, many of the former Office of Ronald Reagan staff returned. Reunited, we remembered our former boss with fondness and worked diligently to ensure he was honored appropriately.

On one of the days on which President Reagan lay in repose at the Reagan Library, we closed the staff office, which was off-site, to go as a group and pay our personal respects. The wait in the line was 9 hours long; people parked miles away and shuttled to the line, where they waited even through the night to file briefly past the president's flag-draped casket.

As his staff, we were allowed to park at the library and cross under the velvet ropes and take our time saying our final good-byes.

It was during that hour when I was able to witness one of the most poignant, emotion-filled experiences of my life. I witnessed an outpouring of feeling and respect from grateful Americans, representing every age, race, and station of life: a service man in uniform, saluting with tears streaming down his face; a mother with two small children, one in each arm, who looked wide-eyed, wondering why their mom was crying. From blue-collar workers in oil-stained uniforms to men and women in business suits sobbing—babies and the elderly—and those representing every corner of the world. The love for this man, again, most of whom had never even met him, was touching and powerful. Their love and admiration for him mirrored the love he had always demonstrated for this country and for its citizens.

Though not everyone has the opportunity to affect as many people as Ronald Reagan did, each of us has a chance to positively influence our families, our friends, our communities, our companies—and perhaps, in some way, even the world.

I want the story of my life to be told with celebration, remembrance, and gratitude. President Reagan inspired my life, and I want to pass along that inspiration to others with gratitude, humility, and impact. What do you want your life's legacy to be?

★ ★ ★

Changing the World

What will your leadership legacy be? Each small step, each decision of your life will culminate in demonstrating the quality of your character and ultimately determine the effectiveness and success of your leadership. By choosing to read this book, you have already proven that you are willing to invest in yourself. It is important to be a life-long learner and realize that there is always more to study and additional ways to grow.

But real leaders invest in others, too. They realize that by building others up around them, it's naturally going to elevate their success and that of their entire team. By understanding the power of gratitude, by being mindful, thankful, and appreciative of those around you, you will motivate, inspire, and give others something to emulate. You will enlist their best effort. They will want to be their best.

By keeping yourself and others focused on what matters, focused on the vision and staying optimistic all along the way, you have a chance to change the world, just like Ronald Reagan did. We have one shot at life. Don't you want to live every minute of every day to its fullest? To leave a legacy that is characterized by humility, integrity, wisdom, honor, graciousness, and competitive greatness?

Hopefully you have seen throughout this book the fact that Ronald Reagan, whether he intended to or not, created a pattern, a formula for success, that we can follow to be better leaders and inspire others.

Ronald Reagan created the vision, he assembled the team, he communicated the message, he led by example, he took action, he handled crises along the way, and ultimately, because of all that, he changed the world.

The true journey to leadership excellence doesn't end here. By implementing what we talked about in this book, it is just the beginning. Just as there was a Reagan Revolution, it now is time for a Leadership Revolution. By following these seven steps, emulating his leadership style and his commitment to principles, we all have the chance to *Lead Like Reagan*.

ACKNOWLEDGMENTS

In life you are only as good as those with whom you surround yourself, and there is a reason why President Ronald Reagan asked Peggy Grande to work by his side for 10 years: She worked tirelessly to make him look good and be successful. I'm blessed to have her as a friend and business partner, and I know that this book would not exist without her. Peggy helped me write and edit this book and was instrumental in encouraging me to write it. She was able to take what I wanted to say and capture it masterfully on paper. She is an incredible speaker and skilled writer and gave generously of her time and talents to provide a historical perspective of President Reagan and firsthand validation of his character. She embodies the excellence of Ronald Reagan and graciously provides a sounding board for me and wise advice I trust and depend on. Creating The Reagan Experience program with her has been fun, rewarding, exciting, and fulfilling. Thank you for sharing your vast expertise, unique background, and boundless energy with me and with this project, Peggy! And to Peggy's incredible family: her husband, Greg, and her four terrific kids, Taylor, Courtney, Paige and Jocelyn, I am grateful for their friendship and for the many ways in which they have supported this book.

I divide my life into two sections: before I met Ron Bailey, and after I met Ron Bailey. Meeting Ron Bailey has improved and enriched my life in every way. He represents the American dream and is the epitome of ingenuity, humility, loyalty, and integrity. Ron entered my life by chance and has become a true mentor to me. He is brutally honest, which is needed and appreciated; is success-oriented, which is admired; and maintains a contagious optimism that anything is possible. The other half of Ron's success has been his loving and devoted wife, Beverly. Over the years I have been fortunate to count the entire Bailey family among my closest friends. Ron and Beverly raised two smart, ambitious, talented, and emotionally intelligent sons, Kyle and Kent. I have enjoyed living life's adventures with these two great friends. They, in turn, married two beautiful and supportive women, Michele and Cristina. Between them they have six terrific kids: Brandon, Justin, Cameron, Megan, Lily, and Sofia. The entire Bailey family relentlessly focuses on making the world around them better—and they succeed! Giving away millions of dollars personally each year in college scholarships, buying computers for students, and donating to countless charities, their lives epitomize philanthropy. The amazing thing about this family is that they ask for absolutely nothing in return. I have never met a more successful yet down-to-earth family with such an abundance of positive life leadership lessons to model for others. It's been a pleasure to see real leadership personified through Ron Bailey and his entire family. The Bailey family legacy is both positive and lasting—and has blessed my life immeasurably.

Otto Kumbar is the type of friend who would give me the shirt off his back, but despite the fact that he is incredibly generous, he also challenges me to be the best I can be. He puts his heart and soul into his family, his friends, and all the businesses he has run over the years. Otto has a brilliant business mind and has a knack for making great decisions. He reads, researches, thinks, analyzes, and dissects every piece of information within a business and can set priorities, reorder and rearrange, and chart a path forward better than anyone I know. Otto and his family immigrated to the United States with absolutely nothing but a strong work ethic and a love for America, which proved to be more than enough. He not only found success and reward here but inspired others to work hard and pursue and achieve their dreams here as well. I am indebted to him for being a great, loyal friend—thank you, Otto, for that. And his wife, Sue, and son, Alex, are both brilliant and kind. And Otto's daughter, Katie, was helpful in contributing to this book. She has a bright future ahead as an author, and I'm honored she contributed to my book as one of her first published works. I am always blessed to be welcomed into the Kumbar home and thoroughly enjoy their company.

Brian Axe, a friend from both high school and UCLA, is a terrific Kitchen Cabinet member who gives great advice and is a true friend. I have fond memories of running the four-mile route around UCLA every night with him, dreaming of starting our own businesses and changing the world. Brian has been a top executive for Google and now is an angel investor for other young inspiring entrepreneurs; he has succeeded both in business and in changing the world. I'm so proud of you, Brian, and all you have accomplished!

No one could ask for a better friend in life than Dan Zarraonandia. Dan and I have talked weekly for more than 25 years since our days as roommates at UCLA, sharing both dreams and challenges. From our weddings to the births of our children, to graduations and losses, celebrations and crises, it has been great sharing all of life with a great friend. The entire Zarraonandia family represents commitment to faith and family, and I treasure the support and positive influence they have been in my life.

Todd Stewart has been a great lifelong friend. Todd, you have built a successful business and family through your hard work. I am fortunate to call you a great friend. I hope you know how much I have appreciated your friendship over so many years.

To Jon Gordon, thank you for the introduction to Shannon Vargo at John Wiley & Sons. She's absolutely as good as you said she was. Also, congratulations on the success of *The Energy Bus.* All of your books are inspiring, and you are positively impacting lives everywhere you go.

To Jon Podany, you are a great friend with an incredible family. Watching your success at the PGA Tour and now leading the LPGA, I'm inspired by your work ethic and visionary leadership.

To Jerry Daniels, you have been blessed with a great family and you are an inspirational business leader. You inspire me. "Love you, brother!"

Thank you, Donald Fisher, for being a great mentor and friend. You helped me achieve success in my first business venture. For that I will always be grateful.

To Chris Clements, "It's a beautiful day!" I have enjoyed watching your success.

To Wyatt and Claire McVay, I couldn't ask for better lifelong friends!

To Brent Barksdale, Daryn Iwicki, Jay Lifschultz, Kent Strang, and Brian Swensen, the best group of friends anyone could ask for. I have enjoyed traveling all across the country with you, training freedom-loving young people to fight the good fight. You are all great Americans.

At the age of 20, I was invited to attend a Youth Leadership School held by the Arlington, Virginia–based Leadership Institute. Little did I know that LI would forever change the trajectory of my life. That first weekend I met the founder, Morton Blackwell, who is the most principled conservative I have ever known. His passionate commitment to the conservative movement and to educating and empowering like-minded young people is unsurpassed. I thank Morton for helping me to understand and articulate the idealistic opinions of my youth and develop them into an ongoing commitment to be informed, involved, and an active participant in the political process. He gave me the foundation to build upon and the tools I would need throughout my life to make a positive difference.

I also want to thank the team at America's Choice Title Company, especially our vice president, Christine Micieli. She is smart, hardworking, and loyal. I am fortunate to have her help me run my business and lucky to have her as a friend as well. Christine not only is incredibly skilled in the technical aspects of her job but she is committed to excellence in customer experience, a priority at America's Choice Title Company. She cares deeply about the business and our clients—and it shows. Christine, I am eternally grateful to you and appreciate all that you do.

The leadership team at America's Choice Title Company gives me the opportunity every day to try to lead—and live—like Reagan did. Thank you Christine Micieli; Clair Witt; Seabron Chad Fears; Jessica Braig; Claire Bell-Irving; Jaime Stokes; Dana Gallen; Sallie Bassett; Mary Beth Micieli VanRyne; Trey Corbett;

Dawn Paape; Angela Haire; and friends Grace and Jeff Maxwell, for giving me the opportunity to grow with you as a team. I'm proud of all we continue to accomplish together.

To Red Scott, a truly great American who left a lasting and meaningful legacy on my life and on countless others. And to the talented team at Vistage who lead an incredible organization that creates an environment where CEOs can build better businesses and become better leaders and be the best that they can be. I am proud to speak regularly for them all across the country and value the interaction and feedback created in that challenging and positive environment.

To mentors and colleagues over the years who have challenged me to always do my best and then strive to do even better: Tim Phillips; Pi, Tina, Bailey, and Isabella Piboolnuruk; Brian Malison; John Jackson; Anthony Zuiker; Ken Hanson; Kevin Gentry; Rob Testwuide; Bob Rivera; Larry Vizard; Gilbert Manzano; Mark Gutierrez; Brian Bauer; Ted Frank; Jeff Tidwell; Rick Brown; Scott Jones; Herb Peyton; Bill Hillegass; Kirk Murray; Jim Black; Kimberly Grant; Geoff Brougham; Christine Lee; David Whitaker; Scott Marshand; Michael Wenk; Don Flora; Janet Westling; Ryan Nichols; Father Steve Thomlison; Kelly Chancy; Meghan Swella; Norma Zimdahl; Will Montoya; David MacInnes; Chris Wood; Tom Reber; Stan Elmore; Les Novitsky; Chris Spencer; Justin Henson; Xavier Mora; Stacey Allaster; Congressman David Dreier; Congressman John Mica; Gary Hollis; Will Pitts; Brian and Cindy Axe; Dan and Jennie Zarraonandia; Todd and Donna Stewart; Jon and Kathryn Gordon; Jon and Julie Podany; Jerry and Kathy Daniels; Donald and Elysa Fisher; Bret and Roshi Peters; Michael and Barb Roberts; Eric and Jeanne Walser; Bob and Sarah Barnhard; Eli and Tara Sunquist; Andy and Robin Mignerey; Adam and Nikki Guillette; Al and Suela Mansur; General Edney Moura and family; Tony and Angi Boselli; Ken and Libby Jones; John and Trish Hart; George and Cara Ameer; Joe and Carri Grass; John and Tamara Harris; Eric and Nicole Haslinger; and Lynne, Nicole, and Jen Westine. Congratulations to the PLP team at Farmers Insurance on the great success of your leadership programs. Thank you to Herm Rowland, Tomi Holt, and the incredible team at Jelly Belly Candy Company, a great American success story. And to the world-class staff at the Westlake Village Four Seasons Resort under the leadership of Michael Newcombe and the life-changing work they accomplish onsite every day at the California Health and Longevity Institute with Tammie Wallace and her team. And to Americans for Prosperity, committed to educating citizens about economic policy and mobilizing those citizens as advocates in the public policy process. You truly make a difference!

I was so fortunate to have incredible, loving parents who remained married for 55 years. I owe everything that I am today to my mother, who raised me on love and optimism. She believed in me and always wanted the best for me. She was an inspiration and salt of the earth. Francis Elizabeth Quiggle lost her long battle with breast cancer on December 29, 2009. She never complained even during her most challenging and painful times. I am eternally grateful that God blessed me with a loving, caring mother.

Without a high school education my father, Donald Quiggle, taught me and modeled for me the true meaning of industriousness and tenacity. He proudly served his country in the Air Force and went on to earn a management position at Santa Fe Railroad.

He showed me the dignity and self-worth that comes with discipline and hard work. I was fortunate to have a father who loved and cared deeply for me and challenged me to be independent and always give my best.

And my deep love and gratitude to Jon and Barbara Sandberg, wonderful people who raised an incredible daughter, Luanne, who I am blessed to call my wife. They have been supportive over the years in every way possible. Barbara is a compassionate, caring person who positively impacts her family and community, and Jon is a great father who teaches us all how to enjoy each and every day of life.

I saved for the end some very special people to me. Thank you to others in my family who provide constant support and perspective: My brother, David Quiggle, and his wife, Staci, my sister, Kelly Quiggle, and all the others who bear the thrill—and the challenge—of having Quiggle as a last name. I'm blessed to have a brother and sister who have always supported me and each other over the years. It is greatly appreciated. They are raising great kids: Ryan, Megan, Spencer, Trina, and Jordan. I'm proud of each one. And aunts, uncles, and cousins galore who have survived a lifetime of my enthusiasm! And Jonson, Kim, and Anna Grace Sandberg, thank you for your loving support.

The Reagan Team

Ronald Reagan always said that his life began when he met Nancy. Theirs was a true love and was endearing to watch. They often would walk through the office holding hands, and nothing would make the president light up more than Mrs. Reagan surprising him by dropping by the office. Mrs. Reagan represented our country with dignity and grace as our First Lady and continued to do so upon her return to Los Angeles. I am grateful for her example of devotion and dedication to her husband and to the perpetuation of his legacy.

Just like there was Ronald Reagan's trickle-down economics, in the office there was trickle-down leadership excellence. I watched the effectiveness and success that happened in an environment of kindness and respect and benefitted personally and professionally from all the people within the Office of Ronald Reagan who also embraced and embodied the attributes of the president.

Fred Ryan, Ronald Reagan's first post–presidential chief of staff and current chairman of the Ronald Reagan Presidential Foundation Board of Trustees, always treated me with kindness and respect, including me in important office moments and significant events. Fred is a visionary leader who always accomplishes what he sets out to do. From serving the president faithfully in the White House, then in Los Angeles, and now from his successful business post in Washington, D.C., he has ensured that the legacy of Ronald Reagan remains strong and lasting. I try to emulate in my own office the environment of support, challenge, and appreciation that Fred always ensured prevailed in the Office of Ronald Reagan.

Joanne Drake has directly served Ronald Reagan and his legacy on a daily basis longer than anyone else. She is passionate about preserving and perpetuating all things Ronald Reagan. She served as both the director of scheduling and chief of staff in the Office of Ronald Reagan and has included me in events such as presidential debates and even the president's funeral. I am thankful for her graciousness and applaud her dedication to carry the torch of freedom and liberty forward on behalf of Ronald Reagan. And if you have visited the Ronald Reagan Presidential Foundation and Library, the museum not only accurately reflects the life of the man but captures the vision and optimism Ronald Reagan inspired in America and in Americans. Joanne was integral in bringing the renovated museum to life and so beautifully portraying his true American story.

Mark Weinberg, Ronald Reagan's post–presidential press secretary, was smart, quick witted, articulate, and warm, modeling the president's wonderful sense of humor, as well as his ability to reframe difficult issues, keeping perspective and calm all along the way. Mark was gracious to share private, behind-the-scenes moments with the president with me, and he always made me feel valued and part of the team. He now does for corporations what he always did for the president—communicate with excellence, optimism, and vision. He's talented, terrific, and a great friend.

To the rest of the Office of Ronald Reagan team who embodied trickle down excellence and represented the president with professionalism, integrity, and efficiency, I learned much from each of you and have continued to carry on what we experienced together into every pursuit since then: Cathy Busch, Kathy Osborne, Jon Hall, Sheri Lietzow, Selina Brownell, Kerry Perlow, Bernadette Schurz, Keri Douglas, Kay Paietta, Lisa Cavelier, Stefanie Davis, Ethan Baker, and Peggy Grande. You were an incredible team who gave 110 percent each and every day.

And thank you to John Heubusch and the leadership team who have more recently advanced the president's legacy through the ongoing work of the Ronald Reagan Presidential Foundation. John is a visionary leader who is passionate about advancing and protecting the president's legacy. John, thank you for your example of leadership excellence, and for being so supportive of me over the years. It is truly appreciated and I look forward to continuing our work together.

I applaud the rest of the talented team at the Reagan Foundation: Joanne Drake, John Shaw, Wendy Withers, Glenn Baker, Melissa Giller, Kathleen Swift, Deanna Baker, Kirby Hanson, Wren Powell, Allison Borio, Barbara Garonzik, Kirk Memoli, Alissa Whiteley, and Carolyn Mente, who work tirelessly to honor the president.

In addition, the preservation and cataloging work of the National Archives and Records Administration is vast and ambitious and has thrived under the leadership of Duke Blackwood. Duke is creative and enthusiastic in his work and in connecting future generations with the lessons of the past. Duke, your long-standing tenure and leadership with the Reagans is a testament to your character and to the value you add. Steve Branch has a wealth of knowledge and was incredibly helpful with archival information and the photograph collection. I appreciate his expertise and applaud his faithful service.

I also want to thank my good friend Stewart McLaurin, who oversaw the entire 2011 Ronald Reagan Centennial Celebration. Stewart envisioned and implemented a historic year of tributes, partnerships, and initiatives that honored America's fortieth president during the year in which he would have turned 100. They couldn't have picked a better representative to champion the remembrances of the life, leadership and legacy of Ronald Reagan.

Finally, I am grateful to the Ronald Reagan Presidential Foundation and Library, which has graciously welcomed The Reagan Experience program by allowing the story of the president's life to be told in meaningful and memorable ways.

And most of all I am grateful to Ronald Reagan, who inspired me and forever impacted my life.

ABOUT THE AUTHOR

In 1996, my wife, Luanne, and I got to introduce our son Justin to President Reagan for the first time. Though our visit was only scheduled to last for a few minutes, we wound up spending 45 minutes with the president, talking about everything from family life to politics. He gave us a personal tour of his office and enjoyed showing us the artwork, artifacts, and photographs that filled it. It was clear that his Century City, California, post–presidency office was a place of deep pride and great joy for him.

Source: The Office of Ronald Reagan photograph by Peggy Grande, Courtesy of the Ronald Reagan Library

B eginning his professional career in the Office of Ronald Reagan, Dan learned leadership personally from the Great Communicator himself. Dan witnessed up close how President Reagan used and applied his natural skills to not only lead the Free World, but impact the lives of individuals around him. Dan has spent his career emulating and refining the skills he observed directly from President Reagan and is passionate about sharing his experiences and those timeless principles with other leaders.

A serial entrepreneur, Dan has successfully started five companies in fields as varied as retail distribution and medical technology, Dan has the hands-on experience to authentically communicate with today's top business leaders. As a graduate of the University of California, Los Angeles, Dan is a company founder and currently serves as president, CEO, and member of the Board of Directors of America's Choice Title Company, recognized by *Inc.* magazine as the second-fastest growing title agency in America.

Dan serves as Dean of Faculty for the Leadership Institute, based in Washington, D.C. In this capacity, he speaks on public policy and leadership in cities throughout the country. Dan has also been a candidate for Congress from Florida and has served as the Florida State Chairman of Americans for Prosperity, an advocacy group committed to educating citizens about economic policy and mobilizing citizens to participate in the public policy process.

Recently recognized as one of the top speakers for Vistage, a nationwide peer-to-peer membership organization for CEOs, business owners, and executives, Dan's messages on leadership and emotional intelligence have inspired and impacted audiences throughout North America and internationally for the past

20 years. Dan has shared his messages of business success and motivation with America's top corporations and associations, and has been featured on the Fox News Channel, and covered by the *Wall Street Journal.* Dan is passionate about inspiring great leadership by sharing effective traits and principles of success and excellence.

Dan founded The Quiggle Group to host The Reagan Experience as well as leadership retreats, corporate training, and keynote speaking that promote growth and excellence in business and in life. Dan provides meaningful, educational components, all of which add real-life value and tangible takeaways.

Dan is a dynamic and energetic speaker whose stories and experiences are memorable, meaningful, and immediately applicable. He spends his life passionately pursuing leadership excellence, continually challenging others to *Lead Like Reagan.*

INDEX